TAKE YOUR CUE FROM THE NUMBERS—AND DISCOVER THE BEST OF WHO YOU ARE . . .

Path of Destiny Number 1
Individuality is you, but don't push so hard—you'll make your goals.

Number 7 Vibration
Yellow is one of your good luck colors and cat's-eye stone stimulates your inner being and brings you luck as well.

Path of Destiny Number 6
Community interests and philanthropic involvement add special meaning to your life.

Number 3 Vibration
Your lucky days are Tuesday, Thursday and Friday, and the 3rd, 12th, 21st and 30th of the month.

Number 2 Personal Year
Team effort will work well; being flexible is more important than being creative.

Number 22 Chaldean Numerology
Lists are lifesavers for you and exercise is an antidote to restlessness.

YOUR
NUMBERS
OF
DESTINY

**Discovering a Personal Life Path
from the Month, Day
and Year of Your Birth**

URNA AND MARLOW GRAY

St. Martin's Paperbacks

YOUR NUMBERS OF DESTINY

Copyright © 1996 by Urna and Marlow Gray.

Cover photograph by Photonica.

ISBN: 0-312-95701-7

Printed in the United States of America

St. Martin's Paperbacks edition / January 1996

10 9 8 7 6 5 4 3 2 1

ACKNOWLEDGMENTS

With love and thanks to our old friend and literary agent of near a quarter of a century, Arthur Pine, and to our precious young friend, Jen Enderlin.

Contents

YOUR
NUMBERS
OF
DESTINY

CHAPTER ONE

What Is Numerology?

IT IS SAID, "DESTINY IS MEASURED IN TIME AND TIME IS MEASURED IN NUMBERS"

We know you will find this book stimulating and amazing. You will discover how Numerology, the science of numbers, came to be, based on the work of Pythagoras, a mathematician who lived in ancient times. The excitement of using Chaldean Numerology, which dates back thousands of years, will use your name to enlighten you as to the many mysteries of life. These are just two methods of interpreting the rhythm of your life, the rhythm of your numbers.

The analysis and explanation of your date of birth combined with your Current Name Used are the keys that provide many answers to the puzzle of the real you. It's not an accident that these factors occurred. The day you took your first breath was the very moment your true identity came into being.

The interpretation of your destiny combines with your character analysis to determine a forecast of your path in life. It indicates your talents, your traits, the total creation of you.

Numerology provides you with an understanding of the what, why, and how of your movements along your Path of Destiny. Your talents and natural traits are highlighted and your birth date provides you with the opportunity to know, through correct timing, when you should expect your life to go forward and when it may be more prudent to sit back and watch your progress quietly. We all want to see our lives as having some activity but there is also a time when you should be patient, do nothing, and be an observer.

For each hour in everyday life's trails, there are presented to you many, many challenges, all requiring some form of personal choice. When is the moment in time for you to choose the happiness you deserve? When must you choose to watch the rain and wait for the flowers that will fill you with joy? The answer to all these questions can be found in *Your Numbers of Destiny*.

Numerology points out the time when your energy may be high and when you should use your talent to thrust forward in the direction of success in economic matters, personal and romantic relationships, occupational concerns, or in the many other issues that make up life's substance.

Your current yearly cycle, the grouping of your personal numbers, also ascertains your aptitudes, and whether or not it is appropriate for you to use the cosmic aid surrounding you to grow and develop. Or, are you in a cycle where it is more prudent to learn more about how to handle your opportunities? Numerology presents a guideline. It is up to you to participate in life no matter what comes your way and know that all of life is made up of cycles—life constantly changes. Numerology assists you in determining which of the many courses of action you might select as you live through the remarkable surprises that life has in store for you.

There are many forces—cosmic, physical, psychological; but what you make of your life is largely up to you and your choices.

CHAPTER TWO

Who Are Urna and Marlow Gray?

Urna & Marlow Gray are twenty-first century Psychic Numerologists, equally competent or skilled at interviewing celebrities on TV, fielding questions on call-in talk shows, or resolving problems in confidential one-on-one appointments, group readings, parties, or conventions.

Urna has a master's degree in psychology and a certificate of merit in human relations from the Alfred Adler Institute in Boston, Massachusetts.

In Los Angeles, California, Marlow had the very good fortune to live with Carroll Righter, world renowned astrologian. He was under Righter's tutelage for two years.

Marlow's stint in the Navy included a four year period of service as a corpsman and also with Special Services during which he entertained his fellow sailors. During one of his performances he was discovered by a talent agent who arranged a contract with Universal Studios.

Although Hollywood attracted him, he chose to return to New York and utilize his expertise in astrology and numerology.

While captivating his audience at many fine places in New York, including the Waldorf-Astoria, the Hickory House, and other famous hotels and restaurants, Marlow had the opportunity to read stars of the stage and screen. People such as Jose Ferrer, Paul Anka, Milton Berle, Eugene Ormandy, Mickey Rooney, and Tom Jones came to Marlow for readings. Often they commented, "He's uncanny!"

In between his work of entertaining many successful ac-

3

tors and performers, he was a male model for a variety of advertisements and catalogues. He appeared in many fashion shoots, as well.

The *Your Numbers of Destiny* awarded Urna and Marlow an important key. They joined forces and became a team. Their combined gift of sensitivity to others' needs is bestowed on a fortunate few. Rarely do we see that gift researched and developed to a higher level. Now, add the vital factor of exposure to virtually every facet of human relationships, and you have the ultimate numerologists.

They guested several times on the Larry King talk show out of Miami and on "The Mike Douglas Show." Together, their work gave them the opportunity to read people like Cher, Red Foxx, Isaac Hayes, Della Reese, and Chuck Norris.

They developed instant entertaining readings using an individual's name and date of birth to explore their audiences' past, present, and probabilities of their future. They became the highly acclaimed Urna and Marlow Gray.

Other than the best-seller *Lovers' Guide to Sensuous Astrology,* published by New American Library, they have written featured articles in *Playgirl* and other national magazines. Their numerological advice to write-in questioners has been printed in monthly articles in myriad newspapers distributed internationally.

The one area not yet mentioned in this biography is a phenomenon. Many people have been witness to Urna's gift. She spent several years developing it doing six seances a week. Urna attributes this "gift" to happening when she was fourteen years old. She believes it occurred when a knife fell from three stories—point down—into her scalp. She began to tap into the psychic unconscious stream and received comments and data to many questions asked by her clients. Her percentages were as high as eighty-seven percent correct.

When Urna does numerology readings she often psychically knows many things about a person that are not indicated in their Path of Destiny or Personal Number Vibrations.

To quote Urna and Marlow, "The next stage of your life is *now!*" With that realization, enjoy this book. Perhaps you will find your own special keys in *Your Numbers of Destiny.*

CHAPTER THREE

How to Calculate Your Path of Destiny, Using Your Month, Day, and Year of Birth.

Your Path of Destiny number is your major number in Pythagorean Numerology. It is one of the most important keys to your destiny. It plots your path through life, defining to you how and why you act, react, and adjust to the varied episodes that complete a lifetime. It can tell you how well a person will get along with his or her family, what tendencies he or she may have, and what his or her goals and ambitions may be.

Using the figures shown in the chart, the Path of Destiny Number of December 28, 1986, is the addition of calculations shown in the first example:

$3 + 1 + 6 = 1$ is the Path of Destiny Number.

The Path of Destiny Number of November 15, 1964, is the addition of calculations shown in the second example:

$2 + 6 + 2 = 1$ is the Path of Destiny Number.

PATH OF DESTINY NUMBER 1

Your Path of Destiny is a number 1 vibration. That is the number upon which the climate and environment of your life is built. Especially for you, there are dynamics

How to calculate your Path of Destiny. In Pythagorean Numerology, all 9s and 0s are dropped.

FIRST EXAMPLE

Let us use the birthday, December 28, 1986.

December is the 12th month—		**1**	+ **2**	=	**3**
The day of birth is the 28th—		2	+ 8	=	10
		1	+	=	**1**
The year of birth is 1986—	1	+ 8	+ 6	=	15
		1	+ **5**	=	**6**

Therefore you have the double digit of December reduced to a   3

The double-digit day, 28, is reduced to a   1

The year of birth, 1986, represents 3 separate numbers (we drop the 9s and 0s in Pythagorean Numerology) reduced to a   6

SECOND EXAMPLE

Let us use the birthday, November 15, 1964.

November is the 11th month—		**1**	+ **1**	=	**2**
The day of birth is the 15th—		**1**	+ **5**	=	**6**
The year of birth is 1964—	1	+ 6	+ 4	=	11
		1	+ **1**	=	**2**

Therefore you have the double digit of November reduced to a   2

The double-digit day, 15, is reduced to a	6
The year of birth, 1964, represents 3 separate numbers (we drop the 9s and 0s in Pythagorean Numerology) reduced to a	2

over which you have wonderful and successful control during your life cycles.

Your nature is positive. You know how easy it is to utilize your sunny personality. It affects all those you meet and with whom you have business or social dealings.

Creativity, if apparent in your number 1 Path of Destiny, should never be ignored because of your bustling daily activity. Whichever of the arts or people capture your fancy and display creativity, those are the people with whom you should associate. You will develop satisfying and long lasting relationships.

Under normal circumstances, because of your undaunting leadership qualities, your personal need to be in the spotlight is only dimmed by personalities who shine in their respective fields. They capture your interest and keep your attention.

Individuality is you. Without trying to be different than most, you just *are*. Perhaps one of the biggest lessons you'll learn in life is to diminish this obvious difference between you and others. They too have their outstanding qualities and recognizing this you must sometimes downplay the effervescent person you are. This will aid you in developing an ongoing appreciation of others instead of losing interest in them too quickly. Your ambition to succeed overcomes your good judgement. You push too hard. Lighten up. You'll get there and accomplish your goals. Disliking restraint and regardless of lucky days or fortunate meetings, it seems ordained you'll go to the "top" in your occupation or profession.

PATH OF DESTINY NUMBER 2

Your Path of Destiny is a number 2 vibration. Your devotion to truth and simplicity permeates your life. The need for straight talk and uncomplicated relationships keeps you steady along your path. You will be reading about the real you and how you walk through life in the many cycles coming your way.

Your Path is one of peace and diplomacy. Similar to the graceful white dove, you wing through life with ease. If you really understand a problem you always can "win" by using your innate know-how to deal with others in less advantageous positions than yourself.

Cooperation is a mainstay in your development along your number 2 Path of Destiny. Traveling new highways on your own or allowing your pioneer spirit to urge you on to different routes is incorrect. It is your Path in life to actualize other's ideas, make new systems work, and see that others are pleased to make changes.

Getting along with people on your Path forward is the true secret of your success.

"No friction!" should be the key phrase for you to accomplish what you should throughout your life. Don't let this lead you to believe you are forever doomed to be a "Goody Two-shoes." No way. It is your destiny to work out all problems with care and concern for others, and when necessary, do not hesitate to compromise.

In any vocation you choose, you'll find when you go up the ladder (and you will), that those before you may have been functioning with a lack of efficiency. You must change the methods of the past to save time and money.

Keep your perfect key to life's path handy. Peaceful assertion will make your life work extremely well without the aggravation many other people suffer down their Paths of Destiny.

PATH OF DESTINY NUMBER 3

Your Path of Destiny is a number 3 vibration. All of your present and future cycles will be deeply affected by your attitude in fulfilling your needs. The ability to meet life head on is your style—this never changes.

As Shakespeare, the renowned English playwright, said, "Life is a stage . . ." and you, number 3 Path of Destiny are there! Number 3 vibrations are lucky people who are the shining lights in a universe that can be dark and somber.

You do not permit the negativity of life to capture your mind and being. You always find the rays of sunshine or blue sky between black clouds.

It is your destiny to bring joy to others, to perk up their morale and show them how to be more optimistic in their ways of life. When you find negative thinkers and people with a black view of everything along their Path of Destiny, it is your work on this planet to aid them by giving hope. Show them how to have a more "up" attitude. In truth, you cannot change them if they do not wish to change, but you can, by your own cheerful being, convince others there are ways to confront problems and bring a new flavor to living.

The gift you have should be used daily. You can utilize your warm approach to friendship and use the patience you have to remain on an even path. You just cannot permit life to be a troublesome journey with no light at the end.

Cultivate acquaintances and friends. You are a born politician, able to manipulate others' sadness to a realistic understanding of their problems, to coerce them gently out of the dire pitfalls of living.

Parties are a perfect stage in life for your merrymaking and the best way to bring joy to many others.

PATH OF DESTINY NUMBER 4

Your Path of Destiny is a number 4 vibration. Self-discipline and a sure-footed approach to life's vagaries aid throughout your cycles. A certain determination to follow a straight line brings you from one point directly to the next. By following your inner voice, you will get what you want.

You are torn apart when life's blessings come too easily. You think, "What's the catch?" There is a deep and undefined need to earn abundance and success by "the sweat of your brow." You feel you must work very hard all the time. You feel you must be relentless in your fight to achieve.

You have this tendency to never let up, to press on always, to find the elusive happiness you crave. Meanwhile, you miss the daily joy of appreciating small wonders: stroking a kitten, smelling a rose, holding the hand of a loved one. You must work on not being blinded by this pressing work ethic you were born with. It's time consuming and requires your mighty ability of concentration to find the "middle-of-the-road."

To aid you are many aspects of life that can be analyzed easily. You can win by teaching yourself to recognize stable opportunities, especially those that have every possibility to succeed by your hard work and diligence.

If your fancy goes to get-rich-quick schemes, all your efforts, your "sweat of the brow," will be failures. Start from a fixed place; the home, a lover or spouse. You need the dramatic knowledge of feeling secure. You can attain this posture if you do not reach out for inconsistent people or ideas.

PATH OF DESTINY NUMBER 5

Your Path of Destiny is a number 5 vibration. You may tumble willy-nilly as you stroll along life's cycles, but you will have fun. The mundane is not for you. Constant change colors your days and months, bringing the delights life has to offer.

Your undivided attention is held by ever-changing situations. The simple, down-to-earth business of life opportunities are not attractive to a number 5 Path of Destiny.

You're like a ballet dancer, pivoting, pliable, and able to move with grace to the music of shifting scenes. Your remarkable ability to face and handle unexpected turning points in your life is a wonderful asset. You can always be sure you're doing the right thing if you reach out for freedom and sudden change.

Fixed personalities or stout anchors that hold you back can be defeating. Others who do not have this delightful changeability in their nature often give you the wrong advice. "Settle down, you're not a kid!" they say. Yes, you'll always have the grandeur of youth in your being. You think, "Isn't change what life is all about?" For you, it is. Seek new and untried ventures. Since you must do more than one thing at the same time, demonstrate your ingenuity with flair. As time goes on your life experience will show you what is worth the adventure and what is just will-o'-the-wisp.

Your sense of humor is a marvelous weapon. Laughter is the best medicine for relieving stress and its influence changes tangled difficulties into clear avenues.

PATH OF DESTINY NUMBER 6

Your Path of Destiny is a number 6 vibration. Often, as you traverse your yearly cycles, you'll move to the "sound of music." If you listen closely, your presence will bring happiness to others. Problem-solving techinques stay with you at all times. You must learn to use this gift for yourself.

Destiny to some is just sitting back and allowing the Fates to push them along one way or the other. That is not the Path of Destiny for you. Your life must be met head on with knowledge from the start that there must be *adjustment*.

The task you have is to learn, as early as possible, that you will never receive what you think you deserve. It's a matter of recognizing this quickly. Always remember, adjustments must be made.

Inharmonious conditions could defeat a number 6 Path of Destiny. This can and will be avoided if you practice your major lesson in life; adapt, adjust.

Opposite points of view can be particularly upsetting. You must adhere to your private policy of listening and negotiating. If you press for harmonious agreement during chaos, you will not win. Using force by coercion does not work. It brings pain and defeat. Bring constructive agreement to groups of people with varying thoughts and they will bend to your point of view.

Community interests and philanthropic involvement add meaning to your life. Use that given talent to demonstrate your enthusiasm to see others' approaches to life and either convince them to change or if that cannot come to pass, adjust yourself.

PATH OF DESTINY NUMBER 7

Your Path of Destiny is a number 7 vibration. Quietly, your strength and psychic ability are a constant source of inner joy. There are many whose lives require others to fulfill their longings. You need to know you are a total unit capable of living each life cycle and adapting the very best of your own inner being.

Your destiny challenge is a most philosophical and analytical one. Every occurrence in the many daily happenings of life has to be fully understood by your inquiring mind.

Ferreting out the truth of what seems to be reality to all others is your task. As a detective, you feel you must find the hidden motives and the "why?" of all events. It is necessary for your well being.

The famous song, "Come Join the Cabaret . . ."—join life—has a mystical meaning to you. Although you never may be a part of the mainstream in life, one of the crowd, you *are* there. Your spirit soars everywhere, indulging itself to fulfill destiny's challenge.

Your philosophic needs are determined by your spiritual growth and experience in practical matters. Not quite total religious comprehension but more, understanding *man*.

A number 7 Path of Destiny is not materially influenced, but somehow excellent economic opportunity seeks you out. Strange, when you are *not* looking for it, it finds you.

By the wondrous mysteries of Fate, you are always protected. Your requirements very rarely are ignored by the cosmic forces. Most of the other eight Paths of Destiny do not have the dire need to rest, relax and get sufficient sleep. A number 7 must absolutely adhere to this important rule.

As well, those who have number 7 vibrations must ponder their own spirituality and apply those principles to their everyday life. But not in a hurried, panicked way. This would carry them into a complicated life and could bring serious trouble. Take it easy and learn that being alone is not loneliness. It's the best road to take along your Path.

PATH OF DESTINY NUMBER 8

Your Path of Destiny is a number 8 vibration. So you're tough! That's all right. There is no one you have to impress. Let's face it, it's your nature. You are very family oriented and will walk through your life cycles protecting those you love.

The root of all evil, is it money or power? The number 8 Path of Destiny must be compared to the person who is vitally affected by the multifaceted *use* of money, by using money and spending properly. It's not Mercedes Benz cars or designer clothes, it is a question of control through accumulating wealth.

To be associated with large corporations and other commercial activities is the surest way a number 8 vibration can be fulfilled.

Creativity, using your imagination, is not a direct route in this Path. It's maturing an idea or concept, putting it to the test of success. If it has merit, it will work. You could almost say a number 8 Path of Destiny has the Midas touch.

One main flaw could exist. You must prepare yourself as you mature to savor the fact that "cash" and financial investments harbor power. The kind of power one needs to understand the laws of economics and be able to adapt them with good judgment without abusing those laws.

It's true, as well, that a number 8 Path of Destiny carries itself along with an intensity that may not be patient or pliable enough. Love, passion, and marital interests are as much a part of a full life as money and power. This lesson you *must* learn. Frequently a true number 8 is not intimidated by lack of romance and passion. When you are ready for *sharing*, life takes on a whole new "business" attitude. You have the aim of finding in a simple, businesslike way the man or woman best suited to live with and go along with your very difficult but rewarding number 8 Path of Destiny.

PATH OF DESTINY NUMBER 9

Your Path of Destiny is a number 9 vibration. The *one* overwhelming difficulty you may have (the only one!) is to let go. It's your main fight as you go through life's cycles. You must let go when time is up. You know when; you will be a happier and a more accomplished person if you learn this lesson as soon as possible.

The remarkable, satisfying "at home" feeling pervades the number 9 Path of Destiny.

Your skills, innate abilities and global-thinking personality adds to the glamour and accomplishment in life.

Your vision is broad, encompassing universal problems of mankind everywhere. A determination is also inherent for you to involve yourself in situations that have stymied others. You are drawn to *culminate, complete,* and *finish* all projects successfully.

To do this, as you grow older, your mental horizons must mature. Stagnating in your endeavors, thinking, "if it ain't broke don't fix it", is not your style. If fixing it brings you closer to your goals, you have the courage and fortitude to try.

It's not unlikely that you'll choose a foreign spouse. Your understanding of others' cultures aids in any romantic liaisons you create or to which you are introduced. You are a man or woman of all seasons who will meander, stroll, hop, or skip down your number 9 Path of Destiny using international or global visits as the major portion of where you will be and what you'll be doing as you go toward your destiny.

CHAPTER FOUR

How to Calculate Your Personality Number Vibration Using Your Day of Birth

YOUR PERSONALITY NUMBER VIBRATION INDICATES YOUR LUCKY DAYS, LUCKY MONTHS, AND COMPATIBLE PEOPLE. THIS CHAPTER ALSO CONTAINS A COMPLETE IN-DEPTH LIST OF COMPATIBLE FOODS AND THE VARIED LUCKY COLORS AND GEMS FOR EACH PERSONALITY NUMBER VIBRATION.

To calculate your Personality Number Vibration, use day of birth:

All people born on the 1st, 10th, 19th, 28th	= 1
All people born on the 2nd, 11th, 20th, 29th	= 2
All people born on the 3rd, 12th, 21st, 30th	= 3
All people born on the 4th, 13th, 22nd, 31st	= 4
All people born on the 5th, 14th, 23rd	= 5
All people born on the 6th, 15th, 24th	= 6
All people born on the 7th, 16th, 25th	= 7
All people born on the 8th, 17th, 26th	= 8
All people born on the 9th, 18th, 27th	= 9

You will notice as you read on, your Personality Number Vibration is closely related to your Years of Productivity and very much enhanced and directed by your Path of Destiny. When you become familiar with all the areas of Pythagorean Numerology, you will be able to construct more easily a complete picture of yourself or friends and family by seeing the meanings of each area and how those meanings interlock and intertwine with all numbers in your reading. Personality Number Vibrations number 1 through 9, and indicate your lucky days and lucky months as well as compatible people, who are those born on dates with whom you could become excellent friends, good business partners, and satisfying lovers or spouses.

COMPATIBLE FOODS

There are many foods, herbs, berries, and medicinal plants equated with each birth date number 1 through 9. I've chosen to tell you a short story of one of the foods or herbs nature produces which is most interesting and symbolic of your Personal Number Vibration.

All others are listed for your information and should be used to enhance your lunch or dinner sometime along the way during your walk down the Path of Destiny.

If some seem particularly odd to you, that is, not found in your local supermarket, there are specialty stores that sell these herbs or dry roots already prepared for tea or soup. You can use chopped herbs to enhance your dressing for fresh salad. Allow yourself to be tempted into buying them. Ask the store manager the best way to prepare your meals using these exotic foods.

LUCKY COLORS

All the colors mentioned in each of the Personality Number Vibrations 1 through 9 are lucky colors. They spark your wardrobe with shades of the rainbow that might highlight your eyes or hair. There's no steadfast rule that says,

"Wear only these colors!" Remember, though, they will be very lucky.

LUCKY GEMS

Lucky gems are described from the experience of those who lived centuries ago. Through history we have read of their uncanny experiences with jewels lucky for their Personal Number Vibrations. In modern times we will find that these very gems emphasize those historical gems worn are correct in the interpretation of the luck they bring. The gems arouse the senses attracting the best possible vibrations from the cosmos around the wearer. They do bring luck!

NUMBER 1 VIBRATION

LUCKY MONTHS

July 21 through August 28 and March 21 through April 28.

LUCKY DAYS

Sunday and Monday. The 1st, 2nd, 4th, 7th, 10th, 11th, 13th, 16th, 20th, 22nd, 25th, 28th, 29th, and 31st.

COMPATIBLE PEOPLE

Born on the 1st, 2nd, 4th, 7th, 10th, 11th, 13th, 16th, 19th, 20th, 22nd, 25th, 28th, 29th, and 31st.

COMPATIBLE FOODS

Herbs, roots, and plants:
Chamomile, eyebright, saffron, cloves, nutmeg, sorrel,

borage, gentian root, lavender, bay leaves, thyme, myrrh, musk vervain, and *ginger*.

Specialty:
   Honey

Grains:
   Barley

Ginger

Ginger, a spice of the East, is one of the earliest known spices to Western civilization and is considered an aphrodisiac.

The root of ginger is dried and can be powdered. It has been used in European cookery for centuries. Its tangy-sweet flavor accents dishes of lamb as well as beef to give ginger a high-rated plus as a special hot and spicy flavor.

Its tantalizing aroma carries its offer of sensual excitement long before the food is tasted. For a number 1 personality it's an adventure in culinary art and an exciting plant to stimulate passion.

LUCKY COLORS

Sunshine yellow compliments a number 1 vibration. The image of brightness and light underscores your personality. It is characteristic of spring flowers such as daffodils, forsythia, and primroses. The look of aliveness, newness and happiness affects the wearer as well as the observer.

Another lucky color is gold. Gold filament threads running through a fine fabric shine in a glorious fashion. A trim of gold braid or embroidery, burnishing a skirt, blouse, or vest allows the innermost part of your being to play a game of shadows, the gold sparkling like one hundred candles.

Even golden brown creates an aura around the wearer suggesting a warm and loving person. It is reminiscent of Sunday morning breakfast toast done just right and flapjacks swimming in maple syrup.

The startling look of bronze for evening wear; perhaps men's formal bow ties and cummerbunds. Women's bronze satin, gliding deliciously over the figure is a stunning compliment.

LUCKY GEMS

The clear golden drops of topaz jewels as they glow and sparkle in your necklace, bracelet or ring reminds one of the fiery splendor of wine. It's as if the captive gold of the sun remains in the topaz. It was at one time thought to heal all illness if placed in wine and sipped slowly. Lucky topaz.

Yellow diamonds, and you will be lucky if you have one, are usually mined in Africa. Its beauty is imperishable and glorifies the wearer. You would be fortunate to wear a ring made of gold set off with a yellow diamond.

Millions of years ago the resin or sap from trees trickled down the trunks and settled in the ground. Then it baked in the earth for millions of years. Amber. The earth was covered by oceans as time passed. Millenia later, the sea cast upon the ground, precious amber. Amber is "electric" as named by the Greeks. Still, the electricity in amber, when it is rubbed, brings a sensation of movement as if the insects imbedded in the amber were still alive, although they have been extinct for millions of years. Tawny amber beads were found in tombs centuries ago, as well as weapons formed of amber. Jewel boxes, mirror frames, and goblets were gorgeous examples of ancient jewelers' skills.

Wear any of these three gems next to your skin. It promises good luck.

NUMBER 2 VIBRATION

LUCKY MONTHS

June 20 through July 27 and July 28 through August 20.

LUCKY DAYS

Sunday, Monday, and Friday. The 1st, 2nd, 4th, 7th, 10th, 11th, 13th, 16th, 19th, 20th, and 29th.

COMPATIBLE PEOPLE

Born on the 1st, 2nd, 4th, 7th, 10th, 11th, 13th, 16th, 19th, 20th, and 29th.

COMPATIBLE FOODS

Herbs, roots, and plants:
   Rapeseed, colewort, moonwort, linseed, water plantain, and ash of willow
Vegetables:
   Lettuce, cabbages, turnips, cucumber, melon, *chicory,* and endive

Chicory

Chicory, a seemingly ordinary vegetable, hides its occult powers in its exquisitely colored flowers.

Folktales claim that the clear blue color of the chicory flower is the transformed blue eyes of a young woman weeping for her lover to come to her.

Such a romantic and lovely story, just your cup of *tea.* If you like, it is a wonderful *coffee* substitute also. It makes a delicious dark brew that is specially pleasing to you, since the taste excites.

LUCKY COLORS

A number 2 birthday vibration is lucky when wearing all shades of green representing the color of foliage, rebirth in spring and the silent power of nature. Even ancient Egyptians used green malachite as a cosmetic; a green eyeliner.

Green, as well, is the most restful color to the eyes. Very exciting, the color green is associated with supernatural phenomena. That's the *luck* for a number 2 Vibration.

Wearing white denotes purity. It signifies a sparkling spirit and acts as protection against all evil thought. White is striking. It can look as sophisticated as it looks virginlike. Perfection for you who holds all laws and truth in great respect.

The third and simplest color to wear is cream, a mixture of white with a touch of cocoa, gray, or blue added. Comfortable to wear in any social environment, your lucky gems would find a perfect background on any of your three lucky colors.

LUCKY GEMS

An oyster, a creature from the bottom of the sea, creates the pearl, most precious and lucky to a number 2 vibration. A special crustacean whose real purpose is not to be eaten as a delicacy, the oyster was supplied to life to manufacture the exquisite pearl. Worn as a necklace it is particularly lucky on the bare skin of a woman, its lustre as magnificent as morning dew.

Another lucky gem for you is called "the child of the dawning day," a moonstone. At the full moon it is said that if placed beneath the tongues of lovers, it awakens true love and passion. Its lovely sheen sometimes shows a mysterious bluish haze billowing over the surface. The fascinating moonstone not only brings luck but happiness and good fortune too, if worn by a number 2 vibration.

The "jewel of Heaven," pale green jade brings wisdom, good judgment and longevity to its wearer. Its Chinese name is "Yu," spiritually carrying an earthly embodiment of justice, charity, and courage. A multitude of admirable traits conjured up for the aid of a number 2 vibration.

Ah, the beauty of these gems; they bring to the wearer all the most meaningful wonders of life.

NUMBER 3 VIBRATION

LUCKY MONTHS

November 21 through December 27 and February 19 through March 27.

LUCKY DAYS

Tuesday, Thursday, and Friday. 3rd, 12th, 21st, and 30th.

COMPATIBLE PEOPLE

Born on the 3rd, 6th, 9th, 12th, 15th, 18th, 21st, 24th, 27th, and 30th.

COMPATIBLE FOODS

Vegetables:
   Beets, asparagus, dandelion, endive, and rhubarb
Berries:
   Mulberries, gooseberries, burberries, strawberries, and bilberries
Nuts:
   Almonds and hazelnuts
Grains:
   Wheat
Fruits:
   Cherries, apples, peaches, olives, pomegranates, pineapple, grapes, and figs
Herbs, roots, and plants:
   Borage, ewerot, lungwort, sage, saffron, nutmeg, cloves, *sweet marjoram,* and mint

Sweet Marjoram

Aphrodite, the Greek goddess of love, was supposed to have created sweet marjoram.

Those who have a happy and outgoing personality, like you, can still use a sweet marjoram oil after your bath. Gently rubbed into the forehead and lightly used on the hair it creates a luscious scent and stays with the user.

In olden days bridal couples were crowned with garlands of marjoram. It was thought the sweet scent near the forehead would bring joy to a marriage.

LUCKY COLORS

Royal purple endows a look of richness and success. It compliments the number 3 Vibration. Sensuous purple, creating a remembrance of the gods of mythology. Most especially Jupiter, who was known to wear purple, was held in high esteem by Roman emperors. The number 3 Vibration carries itself in a stately fashion just like the monarchs of ancient times, proudly parading when wearing this luscious color.

Turn from lusty purple, shading it to an expression of heavenly, delicate Violet. In the Latin language the word *violet* dates back to medieval times. The sublime color is associated with high energy and it is said that it is able to cure those plagued with sleeplessness. It is a divine color, flirting seductively with the viewer's sight.

Crimson effects the heart. Its stirring bright light romances a relationship with spectacular power to attract desired persons. The color, perfect for you, is similar to the feelings of the breathlessness of love, a sensational tingling of the flesh and sexual emotion.

Luck comes to a number 3 Vibration wearing these tumultuous colors of the artist's palette, including mauve. Picture a mauve background with blue highlights on a silk

handkerchief! Or a whisper of rose chiffon dominating a
night of love. Lucky number 3 vibration.

LUCKY GEMS

The amethyst, aside from protecting a number 3 vibration
by counteracting the negative effect of alcoholic beverages,
is a semiprecious stone that has been utilized over the years
as a jeweled ornament in the crowns of royalty in Russia
and Greece. The amethyst's medicinal cures were known
to aid in the treatment of gout and protect its wearer from
bad temper and loud outbursts of maniacal screaming.

One of the more desirable effects of either the rough
amethyst quartz or the polished amethyst is its ability to
repress evil thought and allow great understanding of all
that is knowable. Fear and confusion dissipate when you
wear an amethyst close to your body.

If one is fortunate to find a rare purple sapphire, his or
her luck is guaranteed to be superior. Any of these purple
toned gems bring the wearer the luck he or she deserves.

NUMBER 4 VIBRATION

LUCKY MONTHS

June 21 through July 27 and July 20 through August 30.

LUCKY DAYS

Saturday, Sunday, and Monday. The 1st, 2nd, 4th, 7th,
10th, 11th, 13th, 16th, 19th, 20th, 22nd, 25th, 28th, 29th,
and 31st.

COMPATIBLE PEOPLE

Born on the 1st, 2nd, 7th, and 8th.

COMPATIBLE FOODS

Vegetables:
Spinach
Herbs, roots, and plants:
Sage, pilewort, wintergreen, medlars, *angelica*, iceland moss, and solomon's seal

Angelica

Even you, number 4 Vibration, with your firm work ethic and serious attitudes will love the aroma of angelica.

Not only is it thought to be a cure-all for all ills, but it has been known to have great power against evil. The Archangel Michael was supposed to have come to those in northern European countries announcing this marvel.

Use it lightly in dried, flake form on your food and enjoy its spiritual effect on your being.

LUCKY COLORS

The symbolic association of blue is dignity. It represents a cool, soothing, and orderly person; a number 4 Vibration usually finds it easy to concentrate on issues unemotionally. When half tones of blue are worn they create a look of contemplative charm. As well, certain half shades can embody illusions of emotional neediness, a person who is crying out for love and caring. Although you can at times be lonely and melancholy, you have the facility to use the color blue as a tool, contradicting what you are really feeling. Using tones of blue aid you to change your looks by playing on the emotions of others.

Like a strike of lightning, silver-gray transfigures midnight to early morning brightness. As a star twinkles and glows in a night sky, so too does the color gray enhance the wearer in mystery. When worn by a number 4 vibration, it is a most flexible color covering the span from charcoal gray, using the influence of businesslike attitudes to soft and yielding dove gray, representing peace of spirit and unquestionable love. A number 4 Vibration can create his or her own luck, choosing the appropriate shades according to which way each desires to make his or her luck.

LUCKY GEMS

You are a star! Just like the star-sapphire in a variety of shades of blue. It is a lucky gem, either seemingly cool and soothing or a contradiction between scintillating excitement and quiet repose. The sapphire means "sacred to Saturn." A jewel worn by princes, and in the Hebrew and Persian languages, derived from Sanskrit, it is known to be "beloved of Saturn." It is a remarkable and lovely gem having great power.

Wearing a white sapphire brings a whole new thrust and is a token of luck to the number 4 vibration. It is a sacred stone of truth, justice and peace of mind. How fortunate you are to have the ability to receive the most elusive of all human needs: *peace of mind.*

Buddhists know the white sapphire is a talisman for a happy marriage. If that's in your mind, wear this gem, in fact, any one of the sapphires, and see your luck change.

NUMBER 5 VIBRATION

LUCKY MONTHS

May 21 through June 29 and August 21 through September 27.

LUCKY DAYS

Wednesday and Friday. The 5th, 14th, and 23rd.

COMPATIBLE PEOPLE

Born on any day of the month. The number 5 vibrations are very flexible.

COMPATIBLE FOODS

Vegetables:
   Carrots, parsnips, and mushrooms
Grains:
   Oatmeal, oat bread, and oat cereal
Nuts:
   Hazelnuts and walnuts
Roots, herbs, and plants:
   Sea kale, parsley, sweet marjoram, caraway seeds, and *thyme*

Thyme

As you travel to foreign places in the world in your imagination, you'll recognize the adventurous spirit of thyme.

Its fragrance scents the air on sunny hillsides bordered by the Mediterranean sea.

Bathing in thyme water or using thyme as an oil for massage brings courage to pursue love and passion.

Used sparingly in soups or sauces it aids to overcome shyness. Of course, number 5 vibrations, rarely do you feel "shy."

In olden times, the Scots used thyme to prevent nightmares and capture sleep.

LUCKY COLORS

You have the great good fortune to war all the muted colors of the rainbow. This is most unusual and worthwhile since you can compose your wardrobe of every pastel shade ever created. Pale blues and greens, soft yellow and lavender. Pink and salmon and on and on as long as the shades are light and airy.

Lucky number 5 vibration can also wear grays of any hue from the palest to the deepest rich tones. White is compatible as well, in its glorious clean and bright look. Your hair and skin are complimented by its pristine glow.

You're one of the few who can make your own luck by color, keeping it light and dramatizing your mood at the moment. You know how changeable you are.

You have a tendency to bring vitality of life to the surface. Calling attention to the vivacious personality you were born with.

Unlike all other numbers, you are unique in fashion and can draw upon your imagination to create any mood; all color, very light or pastel, by using gray as its coordinating dark shade for shoes, hand bags, ties, or hose. By creating an optical mix with gray you are suggesting the naturally delicate beauty of a cobweb.

All your colors worn in flimsy textures define the dreamlike quality of your nature. Those that meet you for the first time find their imagination stirred by your presence.

Be yourself, take life's good fortune and wear your lucky rainbows!

LUCKY GEMS

Fate always decrees a balance. Your awareness becomes sharper when you realize that although the entire spectrum of color is yours, lucky gems are extremely limited.

The diamond is the only gem that is truly lucky for you. Man-made copies such as Austrian crystals, glass beads, and the new diamondlike gems can enhance your luck but the real diamond is virtually the only true gem that attracts Lady Luck for a number 5 vibration.

Mined in India from the famous Golconda mines, your diamond is hard and durable. Its exotic beauty is forever yours. Its mysterious and lucky quality is only found when artisans properly polish and cut this provocative treasure from its resting place.

Rare metal such as platinum and silver are particularly lucky for you. Gold for most others, but for you, the elegance of platinum. Its rare simplicity along with silver adorning your fingers and wrists is a siren sound for good fortune.

NUMBER 6 VIBRATION

LUCKY MONTHS

April 20 through May 20 and September 21 through October 20.

LUCKY DAYS

Tuesdays, Thursdays, and Fridays. The 6th, 15th, and 24th.

COMPATIBLE PEOPLE

Born on the 3rd, 6th, 9th, 12th, 15th, 18th, 21st, 24th, 27th, and 30th.

COMPATIBLE FOODS

Vegetables:
    All kinds of beans, parsnips, and spinach
Fruits:
    Pomegranates, apples, peaches, apricots, and figs
Nuts:
    Walnuts and almonds
Herbs, roots, and plants:
    Marrows, mint, melons, mother wort, juice of maidenhair fern, daffodils, wild thyme, musk, *sweet violets*, vervain, and rose leaves

Sweet Violets

Your number 6 vibration craves calm, soothing flower scents. Sweet violets have a seductive aroma suggesting passionate emotions, but under control.

Venus, a Goddess of mythology, was depicted in fields of sweet violets in tapestries and sculptures from the ancient past. It was viewed not only as a symbol of love, but of fertility.

Gentle number 6 vibration, it's your modern tie-in to olden times when life was less hectic and more romantic.

LUCKY COLORS

Your colors are as varied as a lovely bouquet. From the palest most translucent blue to the stark, stunning look of navy, a number 6 vibration has the flair to wear the dramatic or quiet shades of the blue chromatic scale.

Or, you're in the pink! Looking good—feeling great! Rose literally means "pink" in Latin, therefore shades of rose and pink such as rose-petal pink, baby pink, hot pink, panther pink—you choose it, glamour shades or bashful hues.

Webster's dictionary calls pink: "One dressed in the height of fashion, elite." It goes on to describe pink as "the scarlet color of a fox hunter's coat" Colored trousers, worn by Army officers, are also called pink! There are always multiple descriptions coming down to the true meaning, sensuously stirring in a non-aggressive way.

Black, a most sophisticated color, should only be worn for those of you who are in their Years of Productivity or in your Maturity Cycle. Perceptually black disguises the figure; it has a tendency to make the wearer appear slim. Yet it is ominous, certainly not a cheery color to wear since it combines mystery with power. This power can be used for good or evil. You create an optical illusion, but are totally capable of wearing black to its greatest advantage.

LUCKY GEMS

Turquoise, the luscious blue to lustrous greenish-blue gem, were known and used by the Egyptians as early as 4,000 B.C. The jewels were mined on the Sinai Peninsula. Later on in time, Buddha was said to have overcome hideous monsters with the help of the turquoise stone.

Arabs dubbed it the "lucky stone" and it is yours; the ancient lucky stone has carried its weight of good fortune for thousands of years.

The "December stone" is another name bestowed on turquoise. Oriental poets eulogized turquoise as a protector of innocence and good fortune.

It's a marvelous gem binding the past centuries to modern times. Fashionwise it has no equal. Men and women alike should adorn themselves with this lucky stone. Rings, bracelets, necklaces, belt buckles, studs, and cuff links; all to be worn by you, lucky number 6 vibration.

Emeralds! Ali Baba and the forty thieves filled antique boxes with this magnificent stone. It is the most precious color; fresh and dewy-looking like spring grass, yet intense and clear.

Julius Caesar collected emeralds because of their fabled healing power. During the middle ages they were extremely rare and of boundless high value.

The Egyptians called them "lovers' stones" because they were known to heighten the wonders of love. Imagine, not only are emeralds lucky for you but they assure you of love.

NUMBER 7 VIBRATION

LUCKY MONTHS

June 21 through July 29 and July 28 through August 31.

LUCKY DAYS

Sunday and Monday. The 7th, 16th, and 25th.

COMPATIBLE PEOPLE

Born on the 1st, 2nd, 4th, 10th, 11th, 13th, 19th, 20th, 22nd, 28th, 29th, and 31st.

COMPATIBLE FOODS

Herbs, roots, and plants:
   Colewort, linseed, ceps, and sorrel
Fruit:
   Apples, grapes, and juices of all fruits
Vegetables:
   Lettuce, *chinese cabbage,* chicory, endive, cucumber, and mushrooms

Chinese Cabbage

An introspective number 7 personality is transported to heavenly delight on Oriental, green velvet wings. It's a humorous thought that cabbage can create such a fantasy!

When its crisp, pearly, wide, ribs fan out into crinkly, veined leaves, and its undulating borders of light jade green are viewed by a number 7 vibration; it becomes the magic carpet of your analytical personality and subtly urges sensual images.

LUCKY COLORS

As quiet and introspective as you are, it's strange to believe that sunshine yellow is one of your lucky colors. You're so mental and sometimes so silent but yellow has the strong vibration of awakening your most subdued moments into sparkling rays of sunshine. Wear it and bring your dynamism to the surface. It is charismatic for you and brings luck.

Yellow has the highest reflectivity of all colors and is characteristic of happiness. It radiates warmth and brings inspiration to a number 7 vibration by its aura.

Virginal white is sparked by your very being. Usually intellectual, it proves to all who see you wearing white that you admit that you don't know everything! You always give the appearance of an open book with no print on the pages, awaiting the formation of words. Something new to learn, something new to witness and make its imprint on the virginal pages. You are always ready to accept new premises, new ideas, so glow in the rare wonder of all white. A very lucky color for you!

Even green, all shades, again tends to bring to mind the ever growing understanding of all things that nurture different ways of thinking. There is a springtime of rebirth in your demeanor. Your attraction to others is enhanced when your spirit shines. If you wear yellow, white, or green, your presence will evoke everlasting memories.

LUCKY GEMS

Moss agate is as tough as it is formed in nature, just like you. There are secret and hidden reservoirs of ideas and concepts, just like you. It's a descendant of volcanic eruptions! Vigorous at its core, made of microscopically fine crystals that cannot be distinguished by the human eye. A number 7 vibration would be wise to consider having such a jewel as soon as possible.

Kryptos' (moss agate) mineral formations enhance your spirituality. It makes it obvious to those who observe such a jewel worn by you that there is an endless abundance of abstract designs underlying the highly-evolved nature of your personality.

It seems the cat's eye stone stimulates your inner being and brings you luck. In ancient times it was believed if a warrior wore a cat's eye jewel he would be invisible in battle. Perhaps today, the number 7 vibration becomes mysterious and unknown, almost invisible in difficult situations. You are, therefore, not vulnerable to argument or emotional battle. Worn as an amulet, it protects you from evil witchcraft. The cat's eye enhances your psychic ability and awards you with good fortune. Wear the cat's eye next to your skin. It brings excellent results, happiness and luck to you.

NUMBER 8 VIBRATION

LUCKY MONTHS

December 21 through January 27 and January 28 through February 26.

LUCKY DAYS

Saturday, Sunday, and Monday. The 8th, 17th, and 26th.

COMPATIBLE PEOPLE

Born on the 4th, 8th, 13th, 17th, 22nd, and 26th.

COMPATIBLE FOODS

Note: Avoid animal food. Thrive on all fruits, herbs, and vegetables.
Herbs, roots, and plants:
Wintergreen, angelica, sage, pilewort, ragwort, shepherd's purse, vervain, elder flowers, gravel root, and mandrake root
Vegetables:
Spinach, wild carrot, *marshmallow,* plantain, and celery

Marshmallow

Could you ever believe this unusual confection comes from a powdered root? It contains an ingredient that thickens in water and when heated with sugar becomes a paste.

Pythagoras, one of the creators and mentors of Numerology, mentioned it in his writings. He and other brilliant men of ancient history, Plato and Virgil, commented on its stimulating sweetness in barley soups or suckling pig.

You enjoy the idea that others, with the same characteristics as yourself of another age, appreciated this "common delicacy."

LUCKY COLORS

The power number 8 Vibration! The money number 8 vibration! Of course, some of your clothing would be colored purple. For women a monotone of purple can be used exclusively; purple dress, purple shoes, and pale purple colored hose. Powerful and expensive looking, that's what you are. Men can wear the exotic royal purple in exercise suits, ties, or bathing trunks and feel the number 8 vibration bringing luck. The power is stronger and luckier in purple.

Dark gray is synonymous with worldliness. It arouses images of success and stirs the imagination of others. Worn by a number 8 vibration, it reflects the interesting conflict within by exuding a sense of intelligence combined with sensuality.

Very few other Personal Number Vibrations can wear chocolate brown. On others, brown has a tendency to depress the wearer. On you, its earthy tone denotes strength and the manner by which you face the unknown with stamina, meeting all challenges and winning.

Even rust, a reddish shade of brown, is lucky for you. The mood you're in decides the effect you wish to devise by wearing any of the colors that do bring you luck.

LUCKY GEMS

In the category of gems, power rears its head for the number 8 vibration. General Ike Eisenhower, the leader of America's military forces, then president of the United States, received a gift of three magnificent sapphires, two thousand carats each, with the heads of George Washington, Abraham Lincoln, and himself carved into these outstanding gems. Sapphire, the name given to its gorgeous deep blue, light blue, or dark blue color is derived from the planet Saturn, the planet of power. Number 8 vibration, you should consider buying one as a gift for yourself, or tell family and friends it's really what you would like as a special gift for your birthday.

Just as the color purple is lucky, so is the exquisite amethyst. Sparkling purple is the protector and brings luck to those who enjoy their food and drink, sometimes in excess.

The royal purple stone, amethyst, has the magical capacity to protect its wearer from angry outbursts and bad temper, either by themselves or others. Especially for you, number 8 vibration, when you find yourself causing others to make disagreeable comments and unfair accusations. It brings change at moments like this. You will feel more amiable and gentle. You know when your being is not calm and collected. Call upon your amethyst from your jewel box to do its magic.

Both the black pearl and black diamond are rare gems that very few can afford to own. If Fate has dealt you a great hand of cards moneywise, by all means make an investment in either of these exotic gems. Lucky you to have the funds to buy either jewel.

NUMBER 9 VIBRATION

LUCKY MONTHS

March 21 through April 26 and October 21 through November 27.

LUCKY DAYS

Tuesday, Thursday, and Friday. The 3rd, 6th, 9th, 12th, 15th, 18th, 21st, 24th, 27th, and 30th.

COMPATIBLE PEOPLE

Born on 3rd, 6th, 9th, 12th, 15th, 18th, 21st, 24th, 27th, and 30th.

COMPATIBLE FOODS

Note: Avoid rich food and alcohol.
Vegetables:
   Onions, leeks, and rhubarb
Herbs, roots, and plants:
   Garlic, *horseradish*, mustard seed, wormwood, betony, spearwort, white hellebore, ginger, pepper, broom rape, madder, hops, and danewort

Horseradish

The universal and global being you are positively makes you partial to this hot-tasting root.

Your desire to help all humanity, to make the world a better place, is underlined with the use of *horseradish!* It's been in use since antiquity and flourishes in eastern Europe, England, Germany, and the Scandinavian countries. What root could be more universal?

Used in sauces, mixed with vinegar, sugar, sour cream, or yogurt, horseradish is a treat that is global and delicious.

Being the compassionate person you are, its known medicinal properties would be important to you as well.

LUCKY COLORS

Superlative, the color red. Red is dramatic, creating an emotional impact on those who see it. There's no wonder a number 9 vibration shines when wearing red or crimson. Your ability to be a friend to all people, your charm, and the many ways you have of becoming a "buddy" are highlighted when you wear red. It is the luckiest color of all, classy, aristocratic, yet reaching the heart of people, tingling the flesh with your words. All others see things your way. It's a lucky, lucky color for you!

Red and crimson have the unique power to command, grab the attention from all other colors and create a magic that is only known by a person with your personal number vibration. With luck beside you, you can win in red.

Red is said to affect the heart rate. It quickens the adrenalin going into the bloodstream, bringing immediate warmth to the body. In olden times red was considered a key to all knowledge. This is especially so for a number 9 vibration.

Rose is a nostalgic color, bringing you the remembrance of things past that were good and meaningful in your life. The observer feels the same quality, a sense of tenderness and love. Wear lucky rose on romantic evenings and create a lucky environment to capture your lover or spouse.

The lightness of pink is another plus to be worn in the daytime. You look like a dreamy illusion when wearing this color. Your charm and wit can make wonderful daytime jaunts or picnics very special. As opposed to white, for example, your personality blends beautifully with pink, a diluted red.

LUCKY GEMS

You know you can be what you choose to be and the garnet is so much like you—unusual. It can be in the guise of blackish red, wine red, orange, yellow, or even green. Can you imagine, number 9 Vibration, having a wardrobe of garnets, each one a different color yet bringing luck to you at all times and dramatizing any gown, dress, or suit you choose to wear?

Hard to locate but not exactly rare is the jet black garnet and the white garnet. This gem maintains its lucky qualities whatever color. Amazing how you can change yourself; the garnet is really *your* stone.

The ruby arouses kindness and enthusiasm in all people. It's sometimes called "a drop of Mother Earth's blood," and is perfect for you, the lucky ruby. It is one of our planet's most precious stones. The side of your being that retains your psychic qualities is endowed with the gift of precognition when you wear a ruby. It's your specialty, a universal and noble gem that expresses your character and exemplifies your dignity. Most wondrous is the ruby's symbolization of love.

CHAPTER FIVE

Formative Years, Years of Productivity, Maturity Cycle.

INTRODUCTION TO YOUR FORMATIVE YEAR, USING YOUR BIRTH MONTH.

The Formative Years, Years of Productivity, and the Maturity Cycle are based on your month, day, and year of birth. To go into a deeper explanation, you would find it tedious and somewhat boring.

We've attempted to give you a glance of what your past was like from the time you were born on this planet in the personal reading devoted to your Formative Years.

Your Years of Productivity can bring you much satisfaction in accomplishing your career endeavors and those occupations that are best suited to your inborn abilities. In this portion of your Personal Numerological Reading there is a list of various job opportunities that are suited to your Productivity Year's vibrations. You can also compare your individual vibration number with those of famous people who were born on your identical vibration day of birth.

The years of your Maturity Cycle begin at different times and different ways in each life. There are certain ailments that could occur in your specific Maturity Cycle. Although throughout your life, you may have discovered these are your "weak" points and you may have been vulnerable since childhood.

What you will read will be the essence of the way each part of your life becomes reality.

You begin patterns of life from babyhood on. Your memories, genes, and environment will guide you as you grow older. The way you were accepted in your family as a child;

how study and school defined you in another part of your life, tendencies of friendships and giving love; and learning to share—these are all a part of those early Formative Years.

A sense of art will show itself. Your attitude towards music and whether or not you perform all come into being early in life. Some are attracted to pets and throughout life are happy when a wonderful animal friend is close. Others find that being alone is much more satisfying. There's some pain and great joy growing up. Your own vibration will show you this miracle.

To calculate your *Formative Year*, use the *month* you were born.

January		= 1	Formative year
February		= 2	Formative year
March		= 3	Formative year
April		= 4	Formative year
May		= 5	Formative year
June		= 6	Formative year
July		= 7	Formative year
August		= 8	Formative year
September		= 9	Formative year
October	1+0	= 1	Formative year
November	1+1	= 2	Formative year
December	1+2	= 3	Formative year

The Formative Years run from birth through to age seventeen or twenty-one. Each person is different. Use your own judgment as to the year you enter your Years of Productivity. If you're very mature in thinking, you could enter your Years of Productivity as early as sixteen or seventeen years old. If you are really childlike and unsophisticated, most likely you'll leave your Formative Years in your twentieth or twenty-first year.

NUMBER 1 FORMATIVE YEAR

You were born with a singleness of purpose and did not require too much attention while you were growing up. You had purpose to do it your way, even in playtime!

Hopefully, January and October babies, those who were responsible for your care recognized your initiative and independent nature. They should have given you a very long leash to *be* what you were born to be; a person born with independence, originality, and creativity.

It was not difficult for your grammar school teachers and others in the teaching professions to see your self sufficiency and drive.

You preferred working alone and resentment reared its ugly head if you had interference from authority. You knew then, in childhood, how you finished your work before others. You were born with a stubborn streak and encountered some difficulty if you chose to do what you wanted to do instead of going along with others in the class.

Care should have been given to your need to keep working on your own. There was sometimes a tendency to overtax yourself. You never seemed to notice the depletion of your energy.

Even then your ambitions were boundless. Most likely you went on to a higher education or specialized in a particular field requiring distinctive skills which were not difficult for you to master.

NUMBER 2 FORMATIVE YEAR

As a child, you enjoyed playing with only one or two other children at the same time. You were a cooperative student and liked working in small, team efforts.

If you were born in February or November you required

very few other people to enjoy your early years. As time went on you did not need crowds showing their appreciation for your talent. Your own dynamics pressed on for your dramatic quest for fame and fortune. Winning games, enjoying competition in sporting events suited you during grade school years into late youth.

Then and now, your pattern of following the middle of the road, conservative in your thinking and achieving was a blessing. If it was required, you were in the background of a project: "No problem!" From that vantage point, you could see how it was all put together and at an early age you began to have hints of what you eventually chose to be your life's work.

As a peacemaker between two bullies or between the class and your teachers, the group chose you for your in-born traits of diplomacy. You melded easily, then and now, with creative artists, writers or inventors. Organizational skills developed early and became a high point in the occupation you chose in life.

Spontaneity in your makeup was a marvelous quality to have. Anything new that came up, you were for it. Willing to take a chance, win or lose, "Let's *do it!*"

NUMBER 3 FORMATIVE YEAR

Philosophers of olden times believed those born in March or December personified the wonders of nature.

Children of artistic talent and those that would strive for perfection. Lovely childhoods, living in a world of beautiful sugar plum fairies in their minds, loving Christmas time and Santa Claus, even Peter, the colorful magic Easter Bunny.

In your early years it was important to say the "Pledge of Allegiance" in the mornings at school, if you are an American. Important, too, to sing the national anthem of your country, wherever you were born.

It's your nature to be involved in the arts, even to have enjoyed finger painting as a child.

The trend of your life should be one of happiness in your power of attraction, self-expression, and joy of living.

These basic traits never desert you. Affable, charming, and always ready to find the "*yes*" in life as opposed to the negativity. At the time you went from childhood into years of survival during your Years of Productivity, your sureness and self-confidence were a bridge to a great future.

All others do not have the primrose path, blankets of down, to fall upon or exciting yellow brick roads to traverse. Most tread the Path, fighting all the way. You're blessed. Accept it and keep going forward.

NUMBER 4 FORMATIVE YEAR

Many numerologists and astrologers as well consider this vibration a demanding and mundane beginning during the Formative Year of life.

We do not believe that! If anything, the April child has a firm basis upon which to build your life; you are prepared at this early time to reap the rewards that are waiting, for your future.

You have the know-how to deal with the simple, human problems in childhood that prepare you for excellent survival in your Years of Productivity. Even lack of money is not your enemy; if by chance you have it, you quickly learn how to manage it. If you don't, you resolve quite young to learn how to get it! Usually your determination is underlined by hard work.

Naturally, you are always fair. Justice becomes your cause because it's right!

You most often eat properly and on your own admission, candy is not good for your teeth.

Sobriety, concern and factual events steer your ship-of-fate to practical, worthwhile, and meaningful occupations.

Without a doubt, if your choice is higher education, you'll find the ways and means to achieve the funds or position you require for your degree(s); masters, even doctorate titles.

NUMBER 5 FORMATIVE YEAR

Perhaps you were difficult to handle as a tot. Surely your parents or guardians became well acquainted with your constant change of direction and inconsistency in what you thought you wanted.

A special kind of restlessness, recognized in your early youth confounded you and others as you grew into your Years of Productivity.

You're born in May and are a salesman, filled with inspirational ideas. You possess a magnetism that staggers the imagination. Either sex, boy or girl, in your childhood years, made friends, and good pals among the opposite sex. When you "grew up" sex appeal was and is as much a part of your being as the air you breathe.

It's not easy for a youngster to be so changeable. You probably found yourself in your early teens wondering why you kept hopping from one stand to another, from one neighborhood to another, from one "best friend" to another. Your curiosity is never squelched. You learn very young in life that your personal satisfaction comes only with variety in your life.

You are a "people person!" There had to be many in your life when you were very young and are now as well.

The world seems to be a big bowl of cherries, you must try them all or you're not happy.

NUMBER 6 FORMATIVE YEAR

When you were born, the rays of Venus must have been directed onto and into your life. An adorable June baby, a cute little tot and a very attractive adolescent; you were blessed with an attractive personality. Since infancy you have enjoyed raves from others; how *cute* you were!

The need for love and being embraced and admired was an important adjunct to your growth. You required applause from people you love and glowed in the affection that surrounded you. A home and family became an integral part of your development.

To those of the old Bohemian era, and the hippies, you seemed a complete stranger. It was not for you. You were and still are rooted in respectability. Conventional standards such as the right schools, right people, right activities were imperative to a wholesome you.

You are basically a joyful person and enjoyed these attributes throughout your teenage years. Not ever an ugly duckling, you were a lovely swan, floating along with your head held high.

Most people born in a number 6 Formative Year were reared in an atmosphere of peace, an aggressive life just never became a necessity. Good opportunities flow in and you pick and choose.

NUMBER 7 FORMATIVE YEAR

During your early childhood and teenage years it is doubtful you were a very gregarious person. Like most July babies you were overly sensitive and children like yourself find it difficult adjusting to the careless verbal abuse of their peers.

You were introspective, able to sense things that were happening around you and at that time it appeared there was a beginning of marvelous development of psychic ability. It is as much a part of you in current time as it proceeded to grow and blossom without your control. You began to ''know'' without being told.

Friendships were few but those bound to you were loyal,

loving and understanding. Any striving for success in your early years was fraught with difficulty. Attempts at orderliness were sufficiently developed to set the tone for your future. As you grew older, your capabilities proved you could organize your work and life as well. The ability remained with you and grew more pronounced with each year.

Certain words are wonderfully descriptive of your Formative Year. Diplomatic at all times, you were able to get and keep the admiration of your teachers.

If you were silent, it was when you were being receptive. Children could feel this intense "something" about you.

Social frivolities were not particularly required. Talking, philosophizing, debating were your "social" habits in your teenage years.

NUMBER 8 FORMATIVE YEAR

Regardless if your parents were people of wealth or not, it seemed your early childhood was one of comfort and material belongings. August babies are often treated like little princes or princesses. Care, toys, even the position you held over tots like yourself was a time of ongoing "winning."

You could have been an officer of your graduating junior or senior high school class, or maybe president of any of the clubs you joined; you were treated in a royal manner. It was your stamina and effort to be the *tops* in anything you did. Whether it was computer know-how or financial writing in the school newspaper, your flair and understanding of economics grew greater and greater as you matured into your teens.

You always envisioned large sums of money. Not as a miser would but as a very young person realizes the great human necessity for funds!

Every project was, in your mind, on a gigantic scale. In

reality, you have ability to skim it down, but that's how you dreamed. Usually, your number 8 Formative Year Vibration attracted ideas and the money needed for making them happen while you were still in your late teens. Comfort economically was and still is your first giant step to a joyous and successful life.

NUMBER 9 FORMATIVE YEAR

The happiness you brought to your birth parents was beyond their greatest desire. You were born in September, a fulfilling child, always concerned with others. Many number 9 Formative Year Vibration children grew up in homes of relatives and were just as warm and comforting to them as you were to your parents.

As you grew older, the confines of a narrow family circle was not sufficient for you. There's every likelihood you were a teenage guest in many of your friends' homes. Always welcome because of your congenial nature.

In your early and late teens, if the opportunity to travel came your way, you went! The constant change of scene, new people, were and still are the lure.

Riches were not the motivating factor as you matured. It was your overall desire to meet multitudes of people of all professions, a most intense desire.

Early relationships on a one-to-one basis were not lasting, it was groups and then crowds and then multitudes. You have a deep need to be turned on to global and universal happenings.

Cosmopolitan settings were fertile grounds for your growth. Your later schooling could have occurred in a foreign country where you could be nourished in new cultures.

CHAPTER SIX

How To Calculate Your Years Of Productivity

THIS NUMBER SHOWS YOU THE NAMES OF FAMOUS PEOPLE BORN ON THE SAME DAY VIBRATION AS YOU AND LISTS VARIED OCCUPATIONS SUITABLE TO YOUR NUMBER VIBRATION. YOUR YEARS OF PRODUCTIVITY TIE INTO YOUR PERSONALITY NUMBER VIBRATION. COMBINED, YOU WILL SEE EXCELLENT EXAMPLES OF WHAT YOU SHOULD BE DOING AND WHERE YOU SHOULD BE GOING.

The Formative Years run from birth through age seventeen to twenty-one. Usually after twenty-one, the Years of Productivity begin, although they start at different times in life with different people. You can make your own judgments about this "moment," since life's experience will determine when you really know what you want and in which direction you are headed. This cycle lasts into much later years, fifties and sixties with some, and is the major governing factor through your middle and adult years.

The end of the Years of Productivity vary as well with each individual. Living near the end of the twentieth century, Productivity can continue through the seventies and with some people through the eighties. On the average, let's take the year of retirement, sixty-five. At that point most people enter their Maturity Cycle.

To calculate your Years of Productivity, use your *day* of birth:

1st, 10th, 19th, 28th	=	#1 Year of Productivity
2nd, 11th, 20th, 29th	=	#2 Year of Productivity
3rd, 12th, 21st, 30th	=	#3 Year of Productivity
4th, 13th, 22nd, 31st	=	#4 Year of Productivity
5th, 14th, 23rd	=	#5 Year of Productivity
6th, 15th, 24th	=	#6 Year of Productivity
7th, 16th, 25th	=	#7 Year of Productivity
8th, 17th, 26th	=	#8 Year of Productivity
9th, 18th, 27th	=	#9 Year of Productivity

This period runs through many decades of life. It is the guiding key to your occupation, maturing attitudes, and the thrust in your world concerning areas of every day involvement affected by your major key, the Path of Destiny Number.

The Personal Years you are in as those decades pass, changing every twelve months, create the latitude you have in your diversified patterns of living. It shapes your health, love, marriage, in fact, anything and everything that happens along your journey. It's a combination of most of your life, insofar as various numbers have a specific impact on your wondrous travel.

Again, this is one of the most imperative times of your existence. It molds that which you will be with every passing year. The beginning of development during your Formative Years commences to become very vivid in life. You'll find during these Years of Productivity the occupation that can be most rewarding. It's your choice, but you will begin to feel and know what is really best for yourself.

NUMBER 1 VIBRATION: *Those born on the 1st, 10th, 19th, and 28th of any month*

You sense you're different, you are! You feel to do things your way is the only way. There is a pioneer spirit that flows within you and it's up to you how you use it. We suggest you try to use this energy on the plus side as it will attract good throughout your Years of Productivity. If you use this power incorrectly it will attract the negative. Leadership qualities are prevalent. You have a way of swaying others' opinions through verbal persuasion and your actions. There are tendencies of extremism and this far left or far right thinking must be harnessed so that others will understand. A direct ascent up to the heights could bring an equal descent to the depths. A suggestion: maintain a middle course on the plus side. Yes, it's so. You are a leader rather than a follower. People feel secure following you because you do sincerely care for their interests.

Playing second fiddle is not a pleasant position for you to be in. You despise it. Use self discipline to keep yourself aligned in your center path.

There's so much energy here. Remember to get plenty of rest to sustain your active periods. You do not like to be *told* what to do. Maybe if you are *asked,* you will give the direction some consideration.

Someone knowledgeable about your dynamism may take you under their wing, nurturing your training. How beautifully valuable. This will be continued by you, in turn, nurturing someone else by careful guidance. You are selfless rather than selfish.

Since you are unlikely to exhibit great joy in the fruits of your success in front of others, we suggest you have your feast of satisfaction where you can relish it most, by yourself. You know it is "work well done" and can revel in the accomplishment.

Tidiness is important in all areas of your life; home, work, and playtime. Your reputation is of the utmost importance to you.

There are many *occupations* at which you could become a great success!

Corrections officer
Farm manager
Aircraft pilot
Top executive
Jail warden

Flight attendant
Painter
Science technician
Nuclear engineer
Respiratory therapist

FAMOUS PEOPLE BORN ON YOUR NUMBER 1 VIBRATION BIRTHDAY

Woody Allen, actor/director
Dan Aykroyd, actor/comedian
David Brinkley, TV news anchor
Judy Garland, actress/singer
Dolly Parton, country-western singer
Bill Clinton, president of the U.S.A.
Jonas Salk, scientist/physician
Mario Andretti, auto racer
Emily Dickinson, poet
Wyatt Earp, American lawman

NUMBER 2 VIBRATION: *Those born on the 2nd, 11th, 20th, and 29th of any month*

Given a choice of doing something the hard way or the easy way, you tend to do it the hard way! This is so that you can learn and understand from the bottom up. It's sort of testing yourself.

You are cooperative with others especially when they are trying to help themselves. If others are not really trying, you let them go so fast they don't know what's happening.

There's a tendency to over involvement; "all or nothing" of what you are focusing on. Maintain emotional detachment when you are in a position of learning new methods and advanced ways of working.

You seem to attract burdens to bear whether foisted upon you or created by your own desire.

There is excellence in your ability to guide others in their growth as long as they have a positive mental attitude. If you need answers, you seem to go to the top people which does aid you from stumbling into pitfalls.

When you try to control others, which arises from improper guidance through prior teachers, you make no headway. You would do well in the medical field; dietician or counseling. The need for helping others is a part of your personality. The disappointment when you think you are making progress and that person just seems to fall apart again is a blow to you. You have to adjust to taking less of a personal involvement.

Self-centeredness is natural. It's pride of accomplishment. But through self understanding you'll be more effective with others when you try to get your points across. Everything you do is for a purpose without wasting time.

Be tolerant, let people be themselves. It is advisable for your nature. You are an excellent teacher but you cannot *give* knowledge to anybody. If you have it within yourself, a student will find his way to you. Try to give advice and help only when asked. Do not volunteer.

Listed are a few of the *vocations* at which you would shine:

Electronic data processing	Civil engineer
Equipment repair	Hotel manager
Physical assistant	Podiatrist
Nurse	Clerical supervisor
Bank loan officer	Purchasing agent
Drafting	Mining engineer

FAMOUS PEOPLE BORN ON YOUR NUMBER 2 VIBRATION BIRTHDAY

Jimmy Connors, tennis pro
Farrah Fawcett, actress
Mahatma Gandhi, Indian religious leader

Daniel Boone, pioneer
Thomas Edison, scientist/inventor
Oleg Cassini, fashion designer
Cher, singer/actress
Joan Rivers, comedian
Sidney Poitier, actor
Michael Jackson, singer/dancer

NUMBER 3 VIBRATION: *Those born on the 3rd, 12th, 21st, and 30th of any month*

You were born to bring joy and cheer into your surroundings. By birthright you have a positive personality. With these advantages there is a challenge in your numbers to establish your own brand of self-expression.

Quite often people like you are multitalented and should give each of your natural abilities a chance to develop. By this time in your life, it should become obvious in which direction you should proceed to entertain others as well as pleasing yourself and earning more than an adequate living.

Your ability to bounce back from physical illness quickly is wonderful. It is your positive outlook on life that aids you in this regard. You refuse to be ill and it is reflected in your vibrant health.

Many feel that your number 3 vibration in a Productivity Cycle has a touch of genius. If this is so, discovery about this is recognized early. Even you sometimes believe it. The contacts you make and your ambition to be before the public plays the largest role in your life. This display of self is fine, but even if ambition is not your most important thrust in life your natural facility of spreading good cheer and good will in whatever you do will make your own life fulfilling.

You can overcome most defeats; as with your health, you bounce back fast. But when in love, and affairs concerning emotional involvement, romance, or passion, you are deeply affected if you feel rejection. Quite often you choose the kind of people who are not up to your high level of optimism. You feel it's your goal in life to lift *everyone* to the heights. The sooner you realize you cannot change the *entire* world *all* the time, you'll be a happier, more content person.

Charm, grace, beautiful smiles are your trademark. If ambition doesn't stir you on to be before the public, then write! Your expertise and your ability to express yourself so well with words will amaze you. You empathize with sad souls and can reach out and actually make their lives better. A slender book of affirmations and prayers might be your first big seller in the book world.

The psychic world could capture your abundantly productive mind. Discovery of the occult could become your vocation or avocation throughout the balance of your life. The investigation of the veils of mystery that surround life, the sixth sense particularly, grasps your inquisitive thinking.

Your sense of humor makes you a great companion. It aids in healing others. You would make an excellent nurse or physician, a pastor of a church or be successful in any of the *vocations* listed.

Hotel manager	Wholesale buyer
Landscape architect	Meteorologist
Kindergarten teacher	Economist
Recreational therapist	Public relations specialist
Real estate agent/broker	Retail salesperson

FAMOUS PEOPLE BORN ON YOUR NUMBER 3 VIBRATION BIRTHDAY

Victor Borge, comedian
Alexander Graham Bell, inventor
George Bush, president of the U.S.A.
Liza Minelli, singer/dancer

Bill Cosby, comedian/actor
Vanessa Redgrave, actress
Mark Twain, writer
Dick Clark, entertainment executive producer
Jane Goodall, anthropologist
Amedeo Modigliani, artist

NUMBER 4 VIBRATION: *Those born on the 4th, 13th, 22nd, and 31st of any month*

How fortunate you are, you are living through a most worthwhile and demanding number 4 vibration for your Years of Productivity. Concentration, self-disciplined work habits and perseverance are the demands of this vibration. If you will follow this advice as if it were carved in stone, you cannot miss being a huge success in your chosen endeavor.

Many people who have reached the top of their mark are explicit about their methods of great achievement. They claim, and the number 4 vibration agrees, that *setting goals* is the one imperative! When you are set for a trip, your destination is of the utmost importance. In life's journey as well, one should not only imagine what his/her goals are but make it a point to discover the right equipment to use, the proper roads to take and the time element required to reach that point in time; your goal.

A number 4 vibration during Years of Productivity will encourage you to follow a definite pattern. Even if the going gets rough the strength of all forces surrounding you is a constant aid to reach your goals. When one is met, you set another. This is your secret to winning throughout your adult life. Always goal oriented.

There are a greater percentage of number 4 vibration people who are famous stars in all the entertainment areas, athletics and business than any other vibration. The four is so demanding a master that even home responsibilities are thrust upon you and are difficult to deal with most of the time. You live with a double-edged sword above your head insisting that against all odds you *must* be successful. Your work, you feel, is your recreation, playtime and vacations as well.

Rest is the antidote to your stress! Your vehement attitude to accomplishment can be wearing. It's wise to recharge your batteries so that this drive of yours can remain under your own control. Learn the true meaning of relaxation. This means "letting go" and allowing a higher power fill your being with peace which will bring power.

You have difficulty expressing the warmth and love you feel. Yet those feelings are there and are felt. This deep-seated need to have the support and understanding from those you love is the food you require to work at your fast pace. You have learned to hide your emotions and suppress your hurt in love affairs. It is best for those born in a number 4 vibration to find a mate early in life, a person who understands your drive and will be a soothing factor as you walk your Path of Destiny.

If you are a betting or gambling person, which you probably aren't, you cannot win in this lifetime. Don't begin this recreational pastime. Its results will never give you pleasure, just anger when you lose.

It's far better to play your games of chance in big real estate deals, taking a gamble to buy low and sell high. The challenge of the game is that which brings you satisfaction. You will win more than you lose. Your business know-how can be depended upon to encourage the right strategy to make it. Listed are some of the many *vocations* at which you will find success:

Information systems manager	Engineering technician
Mathematician/Statistician	Radio and TV news reporter
Architect	Truck driver
Speech pathologist	Writer and editor
Optician	Painter

FAMOUS PEOPLE BORN ON YOUR NUMBER 4
VIBRATION BIRTHDAY

Charles Lindbergh, aviator
Ann Landers, advice columnist
Thomas Jefferson, president of the U.S.A.
Alfred Hitchcock, director
Liz Claiborne, fashion designer
Louis Armstrong, musician
Walter Cronkite, TV newscaster
Jack Nicholson, actor
Pat Robertson, host, ''700 Club''
Joe Namath, football star

NUMBER 5 VIBRATION: *Those born of the 5th, 14th, or 23rd*
of any month

''Born Free'' should be the theme song of a number 5
Years of Productivity. Keeping appointments are the worst
stumbling blocks for people like you. Perhaps the reason
you get away with so many broken engagements and
missed meetings is that others, who are so much more dis-
ciplined, are constantly in wonder how such things never
bother you.

You've got all the proper cues to finding success in your
life. A 9 A.M. to 5 P.M. existence is definitely not your cup
of tea. Constrictions of time are never beneficial. You must
always follow the path of least resistance to get the most
out of your career and life.

Your need for constant change to prevent boredom,
which comes easily, can be handled in an occupation that
requires traveling. You have an innate sense of color, line,
and style. This enviable trait you possess should be exploited when you consider career possibilities.

You're your own best critic. You know at what level you

function as an entertainer or actor. Often, if you are not satisfied that you are the best in an artistic field, you'll operate behind the scenes as a producer, director, or hair stylist and do a superlative job. As long as you are creating, that's the important factor.

It's possible that during your Years of Productivity life is switched completely from one direction to another. It is as if you are moving on a highway, green lights all the way and then, like a bolt out of the blue, it turns red! Life does treat you like a helium balloon—up, down, and around, but you love it.

There are many temptations to those who have a number 5 vibration during their middle cycle. Excessive drinking, abuse of drugs, an overabundance of gambling with Lady Luck on the arm of others, never you! It's important that these various activities be avoided like the plague. It's not just testing the temperature of the water or spending a dollar or two, it is the ultimate destruction for a 5 vibration with a hidden path, difficult to find, hard to make your return.

You are lucky in so many other respects where people are concerned. You make friends easily, are involved in new and innovative ways of doing business successfully. Social acceptability and a driving force as a salesman makes for a rewarding *vocation* as well as those listed.

Fire fighting
Electrician
Paralegal
Photographer
Cost estimator
Radio and Television
Sports or newscaster
Office machine and cash register services
Management consultant
Paramedic
Restaurant or food service manager

FAMOUS PEOPLE BORN ON YOUR NUMBER 5 VIBRATION BIRTHDAY

Walt Disney, cartoonist/producer
Neil Armstrong, astronaut

Bette Davis, actress
Albert Einstein, physicist
Loretta Lynn, country western singer
Gerald Ford, president of the U.S.A.
Bruce Springsteen, rock musician
Billy the Kid (William H. Bonney), outlaw
Ray Charles, musician/singer
Patty Duke, actress

NUMBER 6 VIBRATION: *Those born on the 6th, 15th, and 24th of any month*

There's a special magnetism to your personality. You attract others and your style encourages them to be your friend. You are desired not only by the opposite sex, who seem to continue to love you long after you've lost interest, but those of your own sex as well who want to learn from you.

There is a part of you that is very obstinate and unyielding when you are determined to carry out your plans. Upon occasion, when you are deeply attached, the caring and devotion you exhibit is admirable.

There's a deep and meaningful kind of involvement that occurs when you are in love. Regardless of the sex of any person, you become protective and overly abundant in your caring.

Sensuality is a fire that burns fervently in your spirit, but it must be camouflaged by romantic moments and tireless affection rather than on-going highly sensual passion.

Your home and surroundings are distinguished by beautiful objects of art. Rich color, paintings oftentimes created by your own brush and the sound of music brings great happiness to every day living.

An underlying anger is always ready to overtake you when you allow it. You will not put up with opposition and will fight endlessly in ardent argument for ideas, projects and people who, in your opinion, deserve your protection. The fact is, you are basically an idealist and foolishly look for perfection. This, of course, is rarely realized in life.

What an excellent actor you could be in the theater, on TV, or on the radio. The field of interior design would be a superior profession for your middle cycle or any one of the *vocations* listed:

Commercial or graphic artist	Musician
Cook/chef	Editor/writer
Food scientist	Home health aid
Labor relations specialist	Operations manager
	Psychologist

FAMOUS PEOPLE BORN ON YOUR NUMBER 6 VIBRATION BIRTHDAY

Sigmund Freud, psychoanalyst
Ira Gershwin, lyricist
Andy Warhol, artist
Julia Child, chef
Oscar Peterson, jazz musician
Neil Diamond, songwriter/singer
John Belushi, actor/comedian
Nancy Reagan, former first lady
Martin Luther King, Jr., civil rights leader

NUMBER 7 VIBRATION: *Those born on the 7th, 16th, and 25th of any month*

Many numerologists consider the number 7 vibration, especially during the Years of Productivity, a "sacred gift." There is no other number vibration that dwells as deeply in life's cosmic questions and answers as the seven.

You have a constant struggle against all odds. You are a good person and work diligently, still you do not find that which you are seeking. It will only happen when Fate, the purest of all mental concepts, tips the scales in your favor. It does happen! One must have deep faith and be patient. During the battle of survival, develop those parts of self that blend with all spiritual segments of life. So "smell the flowers," "walk in the rain;" nature will constantly renew you.

All partnerships of a number 7 vibration must be built on a spiritual foundation. Follow your own intuition and inventive genius. You will be productively creative, living in a world of ideas and ideals *and* making them happen. There's a great possibility of your face being projected on a movie or television screen. You could as well be the scientist to find a cure for AIDS!

Through the spiritual basis of your nature, there's a preponderance of dealing in the psychic world as a medium or automatic writer. There are a few number 7 vibration people whose telekinetic work has been photographed in Russia. They have the sensory ability to move small objects with their minds!

You are filled with all kinds of talent. Performing before the public, being a giant in business, a quoted, famous philosopher, or a renowned dancer. You name it, a number 7 vibration can do it. There is success in many fields awaiting you.

One of the most amazing facets of your personality is an ability to feel love very deeply, especially for family. Also, you have the miraculous power to hide your deepest feelings if you wish to do so. When number sevens turn their back on people, there are rarely second chances given to renew or rebuild relationships.

Consider the *vocations* listed as, "Any one of them and I'll make my mark!"

Agricultural scientist   Administrative assistant
Corrections officer   Chemist

Flight engineer
Computer systems analyst
Jail warden
Sheet metal worker

Employment interviewer
Health services administrator

FAMOUS PEOPLE BORN ON YOUR NUMBER 7 VIBRATION BIRTHDAY

James Garner, actor
Billy Graham, evangelist
Gloria Steinem, journalist/feminist leader
Ella Fitzgerald, jazz singer
Al Pacino, actor
Ringo Starr, Beatles
Sonny Bono, singer/politician
Liberace, pianist/singer
Sean Connery, actor
Iman, supermodel

NUMBER 8 VIBRATION: *Those born on the 8th, 17th, and 26th of any month*

The number 8 vibration relates to and lends aid to the power of possessions and material wealth! If you are fully aware of this marvelous facility that comes with your birth there is no question money problems will never plague you. One must be able to recognize this splendid opportunity during your number 8 vibration Years of Productivity.

Because of this cosmic relationship to your birth vibration you must master the mysteries of finance. The inborn ability to know when to invest and when to "pass" is there. It is your desire to be on the receiving end of assets that can bring you and those you love the aid, the comforts and security of having funds for every need.

Having this vibration makes serious demands on your love relationships. Too often a man or a woman will marry for money goals. This method does not hold up throughout life. It requires that person to be solely independent in the methods by which they acquire financial stability. Frank Sinatra, when he sings, "I did it my way," proves an ominous but important lyric for a number 8 vibration.

This is a perfect influence for bankers, brokers, or financiers. It is a blessing to have a money consciousness. You would do well as the head of your own business or a partnership in a large corporation guiding their fate on Wall Street.

You've learned or will learn during this important cycle in your life to commercialize your talents to your best advantage. Whether it be in the arts or business, politics or government, you are efficient and able to make your projects pay off.

It's so marvelous to know that it's up to you to maintain your high level of concentration into your Maturity Cycle whereby you will earn rewards straight through to your eighties or nineties.

For an example, one of the most famous and notorious stars of all time was born on your vibration day—Elvis Presley. Not only did he change the style of music the world came to love, but he made multi-millions doing it. Even though he had his own share of failure or disappointment, his charisma, talent and date of birth continues to bring celebrity and fortune to his heirs more than a decade after his death.

There are many positions and *vocations* worthwhile for a number 8 vibration.

Financial manager
Agricultural scientist
Stock brocker
Diesel mechanic
Military officer
Insurance underwriter

Management consultant
Securities and financial
    services
Men's hair stylist
Corporate controller

FAMOUS PEOPLE BORN ON YOUR NUMBER 8 VIBRATION BIRTHDAY

Hillary Clinton, first lady
Paul Newman, actor
George Gershwin, composer
David Bowie, singer/songwriter
Barbara Bush, former first lady
Reverend Jesse Jackson
Melissa Gilbert, actress
Muhammad Ali, boxer
Davy Crockett, frontiersman
Diana Ross, singer

NUMBER NINE VIBRATION: *Those born on the 9th, 18th, or 27th of any month*

The number 9 vibration can be far reaching, bringing the glamour and excitement you cherish into your life. It's a number of global interest, inviting success with all cultures, ethnic agreements and gigantic deals. We will admit it operates on different sliding scales. If your motivation during your Formative Years was such that you thrived on learning the habits, languages and history of foreign countries, you are headed in these Years of Productivity to garner the best from intercontinental vibrations. If it was less than that, your studies could have aroused deep humanitarian exploits to feed a hungry world.

There is a preponderance in your life for long and rewarding journeys. You have a childlike excitement that never leaves you, to go and see and do *elsewhere;* every place but at home. The wanderlust is not a loose, restlessness that overcomes you, it's seeing how, knowing what, and doing large projects all over the world.

Do not start too many new things at any one particular

time in your life. It's important to culminate an endeavor, see it work as you envisioned it in the large picture before you go on to your next "production." We use the word production advisedly. Nothing you do is small, on a temperate scale. It's large, involving many who need your firm involvement to work out all angles to compliment the entire enterprise.

You could also find great happiness in managing others' huge fortunes. The need for you to function independently is seen by many quite clearly. The truth in this situation is that you must become "the man" or the woman who runs the show! It isn't ego that prevents you from joining others to make big successes, it's an innate knowledge that you know how! Your elastic mind stretches beyond that of the average person. You do think broader, further and conclusively without input from less or smaller thinking individuals.

There are many *vocations* that would suit your number 9 vibration.

Geologist and geophysicist
Ophthalmic labortaory tech
Travel agent
Court reporter
Ancient arts administrator
Farm manager

Real estate broker
Registered nurse
Veterinarian
Educational administrator

FAMOUS PEOPLE BORN ON YOUR NUMBER 9 VIBRATION BIRTHDAY

Whitney Houston, singer
Billy Joel, singer/songwriter
Candice Bergen, actress/comedian
Carl Sagan, scientist

John Lennon, Beatles
Steven Spielberg, film director
Elizabeth Taylor, actress
Mikhail Baryshnikov, ballet dancer
Helen Keller, advocate for the handicapped

CHAPTER SEVEN

How to Calculate your Maturity Cycle.

KNOWLEDGE OF YOUR MATURITY CYCLE CAN BRING GREAT JOY AND UNDERSTANDING OF THE LATER YEARS OF YOUR LIFE.

To calculate your Maturity Cycle, use the year of birth, dropping the 9s and 0s as follows:

1918	=	1	+	1	+	8	=	10	= #1 Maturity Cycle
1928	=	1	+	2	+	8	=	11	
				1	+	1	=	2	= #2 Maturity Cycle
1938	=	1	+	3	+	8	=	12	
				1	+	2	=	3	= #3 Maturity Cycle
1948	=	1	+	4	+	8	=	13	
				1	+	3	=	4	= #4 Maturity Cycle
1958	=	1	+	5	+	8	=	14	
				1	+	4	=	5	= #5 Maturity Cycle
1950	=			1	+	5	=	6	= #6 Maturity Cycle
1960	=			1	+	6	=	7	= #7 Maturity Cycle
1934	=	1	+	3	+	4	=	8	= #8 Maturity Cycle
1926	=	1	+	2	+	6	=	9	= #9 Maturity Cycle

Some will choose to continue their careers as formed during their Years of Productivity. Others will desire complete release, doing all those things they never had time to accomplish in the past. Some will find travel, new people, seeing new places, the stimulus to keeping life meaningful.

Recognizing that, be aware of stamina and health and arrange participation accordingly.

NUMBER 1 MATURITY CYCLE

"Life begins at forty!" no longer has true meaning. The population in current times in our history befuddles the olden day thinkers. *Any age* is capable of making life new again.

A number 1 Maturity Cycle puts you back into a position of leadership. Leading your own life in an independent, even solitary way, can be handled, if necessary.

There are many others who need to see how you manage to keep current with the news and get involved in the world in which you are living.

Perhaps in the past you marched in parades to Washington, D.C. or in your home town to object strenuously to some national policy that was unsuitable in your mind. Today, maybe that march would tire you, but you can write your representatives, to let them all know your feelings. You can phone your friends, or aid the cause by asking the leaders how you can help.

A number 1 vibration can now take the "bull by the horns." If it's listening to symphonies, going to museums or reading all those books you missed during your life, *now* is the time to do it.

Visit others who do not have your vital health and need company, not just for chit-chat, but to hear words of hope. Let them know that a change of attitude toward their own positions in life can make the big difference.

Many people who live in a number 1 Maturity Cycle can help younger people manage and operate a small business. As the leader you are, the experience you've garnered gives you the ability to consult with others who desire to make their new businesses prosper.

NUMBER 2 MATURITY CYCLE

Most people in their sixties, seventies, and eighties have the ability to stay with the times. They recruit the past only as a pointer toward the *now* of life.

The special knowledge you already have is *knowing* that the Maturity Cycle is the tying together of life's experience, the lessons learned through trial and error. The bottom line is the *now*.

You were always a people person. You demanded the best from yourself by learning the entire process of whatever you were involved in during your Years of Productivity.

Don't stop now! Be there as you always were to show others the shortcuts to accomplishing their goals.

You have a particularly fine ability to aid teenage children, and to encourage them along the proper productive paths in life. Take the opportunity to counsel those who are really off the beaten path to get back on and to learn their work whether they become truck drivers, bakers, or executives in a large corporation. You know the basics of all success. Let your own experience aid these children.

A number 2 vibration has the need to be there when needed. Take one day a week, two or three hours a day, to work in a hospital or clinic teaching new mothers and fathers how to deal with their pre-school children.

Or you can take the time now not only to write your memoirs for your own pleasure and understanding, but to leave as a legacy to those you love.

Give again! Give with all you have acquired over the years. People need you.

NUMBER 3 MATURITY CYCLE

An unselfish wholesomeness surrounds your giving. All of us searched throughout the years for that special something. It comes to you, if you allow it, and finally satisfies your search, the striving to *know*.

There you are again. Enjoying the number 3 flair of your Maturity Cycle. You've performed in the past, you've learned how and why a performance before the public works and why it doesn't.

Coach aspiring young performers. Rather than bore them with your past achievements, show them how! Let them partake of your knowledge.

Maybe during those Years of Productivity you dreamed of being a Director. Now is the time to try your hand. High schools and middle schools need help when the dramatic club, the chorus, or dancers are ready to perform for their peers. Your presence in a number 3 Maturity Cycle brings smiles of joy to others. Try yourself to *see* that your attitude picks up the vibrations of this best part of your life.

Radio, public speaking; any part of your life's experience can be exploited. Put yourself *there*, you do know how. Those things we never forget.

NUMBER 4 MATURITY CYCLE

You're still busy living life to the fullest and love it. Others may retire when they're in their sixties, but not you. Everyone *knows* you're going to work and contribute to society until the "last gun is fired," until "the fat lady sings," and until you, personally, are ready to hang up your spurs.

A worker like you've always been acquires renewed dynamics in your number 4 Maturity Cycle.

Exercise too, keeps that body of yours in the best shape possible. Jogging is out, walking is in. Do it. Find a safe place to walk each day of your life. Although you never were a people person that much, animals always gave you joy and happiness.

Take the animals of friends and neighbors for a walk on your daily journeys. You'll love the companionship of man's best friend.

You always had a prioritylike duty to others. It was so important during your Years of Productivity. This will never change, but your attitude should; duty to *yourself* should be fulfilled as you desire during this Maturity Cycle.

NUMBER 5 MATURITY CYCLE

This particular Maturity Cycle number 5 brings forward all those desires for change you thought you needed throughout your life. This is the time.

Flit from flower to flower taking the honey for yourself. Try anything you've put aside for the need to get out there and work.

Taste the joys of freedom.

Re-decorate your home, whether it's a new covering for a chair or an object of art you always wanted; do it.

Read those "how-to" books. They claim, "You too can be a millionaire at sixty." Why not? It'll give you a hand in actually garnering your first million or better still, you'll have plenty of laughs.

One area you must watch; spend your money wisely and carefully. A number 5 Maturity Cycle is like a heady wine. You may feel like the famous "Diamond Jim." Spend, but frugally. It really takes little to bring you joy.

The aquarium nearby or in a larger city is waiting for you. It's a mind-boggling avocation to learn about water-world creatures. Watching huge fish, mammals like whales or porpoises, and listening to them talk to each other, is really enlightening and fun. Just watching their pranks will give you many chuckles, and help you learn about them. Their habits and odd ways are not only educational, but something you've never seen.

The key words during a number 5 Maturity Cycle is keep busy and enjoy yourself.

NUMBER 6 MATURITY CYCLE

Although you were idealistic in your early youth, disenchantment hounded you. But now you can believe again and life can commence to bear fruit due to you. Your basic being has always required a sharing with others. There will be time now to be with and enjoy many you have always loved and admired. You will be there for their support and they will applaud your kind nature.

This is such a marvelous time in your life and you may decide to make a big move from your current residence. Even moving to a different city or state. Don't hesitate, it may mean the big difference you've longed for. There were many years you didn't make a change because you "couldn't" leave for one reason or another. There's only one important factor to consider. In a number 6 Maturity Cycle it is helpful if there are people you know living in this new direction in which you are headed—family or old friends who have already made the move. If that's not possible, change from one part of your town or city to another. Do what your inner voice tells you to do. Listen carefully to that voice; it will not push you in the wrong direction.

NUMBER 7 MATURITY CYCLE

A number 7 Maturity Cycle is one that represents the most important phase of a complete understanding of self.

Throughout your Years of Productivity you were too busy achieving or spending much of your private time figuring the best strategy *to win* on each event that came into your life, and you did.

The *now* brings you the peace of mind that comes with full understanding. There's a poignant feeling that stirs up memories of the past but allows the structuring of what is to be.

If you wish to continue to work at any occupation, as most number 7 Maturity Cycles do, it would be advantageous to deal with a spiritual involvement you deem possible.

Of all things, working in an administration area at your local zoo provides a fund of information and involvement with people who care about animals. This is surely a spiritual area of life.

There are programs for those who are "quitting" drugs. A mature person who wants to help can contribute a great deal to these programs as a volunteer. Or you could get involved with the world of parapsychology. A library in most cities has a multitude of books to explain as well as tell histories and tales about this magical part of life. You can begin to learn about this mysterious realm.

You'll find yourself having psychic incidents occur. For example, knowing the phone will ring and it does, or expecting a visit from someone you haven't heard from for years, and they show!

As you learn more about a number 7 Maturity Cycle you'll find a whole new world to explore. It's captivating. This new dimension of life can open for you and it brings much understanding of those episodes you do not hear or see, but feel.

NUMBER 8 MATURITY CYCLE

This number 8 Maturity Cycle is most interesting. There are many words we could have chosen other than "interesting," but a number 8 is that!

You are placed in a position whereby you will continue to work diligently and full-time for many more years after age sixty-five. The need to continue "earning your bread" is not the reason. Most likely you have accumulated enough to stop and play; enjoy money to have good times.

It's not easy to do this in a number 8 Maturity Cycle. There is an obsessive need to continue your path along the same roads and byways you used during your Years of Productivity. It's useless to make suggestions to you of other ways to spend your free time. You want to and like working or you would not do so. There's no question it could be very rewarding.

One important bit of advice you should heed is something you usually put aside during your life. It is advisable to get annual check-ups from your physician. You are headstrong and will not accept the fact you could be doing too much. At any time in life, exhaustion can creep up on you. Abide and accept this wisdom and all will be as you "will" it.

Remember, you are not a slave. No one is cracking a whip to see that you do not falter. It's all right to slow down your pace and still get the same rewards.

NUMBER 9 MATURITY CYCLE

This is a wonderful Maturity Cycle, the number 9. It provides all the opportunity you need to travel when you wish. To aid others who need your expert advice about survival and to explore all the unknowns about yourself. A trip to the library could open up new avenues of interest and spark ideas to put into action. Information you glean from ''self-help'' books, can be passed on to people who cross your path and need uplifting.

There are so many corners of yourself to discover, so many avocations to capture your fancy and keep your mind alert. Take good advantage of this time.

Have your eyes examined periodically so that you can either learn or continue to drive. Being mobile can open up your horizons to travel and enjoy life. Take in nature's beauty and revel in the wonderment of creation.

There is a panorama spread before you. Glimpses of a world that will bring you great joy during your Maturity Cycle.

CHAPTER EIGHT

How to Calculate the Universal Year and Your Personal Year.

YOU WILL HAVE AN AWARENESS OF THE MOVEMENT IN YOUR FINANCES AND CAREER, FRIENDSHIP AND FAMILY, ROMANCE AND LOVE, HEALTH, AND OTHER GUIDELINES.

UNIVERSAL YEAR

This year is 1996 for the world. Therefore, the Universal Year is $1 + 6 = 7$. The world is in a number 7 year.

PERSONAL YEAR

To calculate your Personal Year of Numerology's 1 through 9 year life cycle, use your birthday:

1. For birthdate: July 7, 1961

$$\begin{array}{l} \#7 \text{ (Universal year)} \\ \#7 \text{ (July—month born)} \\ \underline{+\ \#7 \text{ (day born}} \\ \#21 \rightarrow \#2 + \#1 = \#\ 3 \end{array}$$

You are in a #3 year of your 9-year life cycle.

2. For birthdate: February 13, 1978

$$\begin{array}{l} \#7 \text{ (Universal year)} \\ \#2 \text{ (February—month born)} \\ \underline{+\ \#4 \ (1+3=4\text{—day born)}} \\ =\#13 \rightarrow \#1 + \#3 = \#\ 4 \end{array}$$

You are in a # 4 year of your nine-year life cycle.

When you reach your Personal Year number 9, you *know* the following year you enter a number 1 Personal Year again to begin your new nine-year life cycle.

NUMBER 1 PERSONAL YEAR

FINANCES AND CAREER

This year marking time is over, there's a big thrust forward, giving your career a shot in the arm. A number 1 Personal Year of new beginnings is expressly perfect to make new patterns at work, new approaches, and an upswing in your finances. Start out this cycle correctly; look for better and newer ways to make your business or career operate far more efficiently than ever before.

There will be new opportunities coming your way and awareness of them is of primary importance. This doesn't mean that every new possibility that crosses your desk is the key to your Destiny. Carefully examine each one, you'll know which to pursue.

Search out new contacts, enlarge your circle of friends and associates. Find every and any avenue to market yourself to attract new business involvement. Don't take "no" for an answer.

Wipe the cobwebs out of your mind and allow your natural creativity to take hold, to change old ways of functioning to new. Consider your current job. Are you earning your worth? Figure it out. If your company is in fiscal shape, go for it! Ask for a raise in pay. Go to your direct supervisor, if you are not successful there tell him or her, "I'm going up the next step, your *boss*." Request your supervisor's permission to do so. Either way, whether you get their okay or not, do it. Very nicely and without being greedy, do it!

FRIENDSHIP AND FAMILY

Although there may have been dissension in the past, in a new cycle it's gone. Family is waiting to hear from you. It's a new chance to make your blood relations a closer part of your life. Invite them over for a simple snack or barbecue. Mend old differences among cousins, aunts, and uncles. If arranging little get-togethers doesn't suit you just yet, sit down and make a series of phone calls. Let all know you're feeling great and want to stay in touch.

It's difficult for people to make the first contact after a period of time. Sometimes embarrassing, but *you* do it. Afterwards, you'll feel closer to the joys of living amongst your relatives again. Try it, this is the year to make a new effort; be sincere and you will feel fulfilled.

When we're feeling great, we chuckle at the memories of friends we used to enjoy and admit we miss those people; this again is the year to renew old acquaintances and develop other people around you who have the same interests as yourself.

Maybe your office pal can become more a part of your life. Invest in a Sunday afternoon picnic or visit. She or he will have friends there, you'll have an opportunity to meet a whole new parcel of people. If you find one person, it's a plus adding a great new flavor to your life.

Perhaps old friends who live far away are thinking about you. Resume your letter writing, tell them what's happening and how you insist they stay in touch. It will add dimensions to your life.

ROMANCE AND LOVE

In the past you started to take your spouse or lover for granted. Think about that now, very seriously. It is really over? Do you feel you and your mate or "most significant other" should really call it quits? If you decide you just lost touch with each other, you must work at your relationship a little harder or its time to talk and discuss dissatisfactions. Don't give up. This year try to re-establish those old feelings. You were in love once.

With careful thought and love, not anger, if it's really over, start your campaign to find that perfect someone for yourself.

Let it be known around that you're available again. Accept all social invitations even to those places you failed to go in the recent past. Join a new hobby group. The people there have similar interests as you. Meeting others this year could have a dual purpose; a new friend or lover.

HEALTH

In a brand new Cycle, one feels marvelously alive. There is a surge of good feeling physically and mentally.

If you've been putting off a medical check-up, start the new Cycle with a "seal of approval" from your physician. Make everything you deal with this year, new. Resolve to exercise more; and do it. Eat properly avoiding fats, cholesterol and fried foods. It's no longer stylish to be sedentary, so do something, whether it's aerobics or just long walks. At this new juncture in your life, whatever you choose will be rewarding if you follow through.

GUIDELINES

If you commence with a flash to nurture new business actively and let it hang by dashing away before you've really done a job, you'll find all your efforts are self-defeating. Stay with it, don't let down.

It would be wise if you guard yourself about being *overly* optimistic.

Concerning a much better love life, keep on an even keel. Vacillating on or off about looking for someone new is not in your best interest.

The honest thought you give to maintaining your present involvement must, at this time, be put into action. No self-doubt. No expectation of winning without compromise. Work together to make your new Cycle work, bringing back the love and attention you crave.

Above all, be firm when you know you are right. You will remain in this Personal Year until your next birthday.

NUMBER 2 PERSONAL YEAR

FINANCES AND CAREER

We've indicated throughout your Personal Numerological Reading that life continually changes; good times, not so good times, and so on. In a number 2 Personal Year, your life should start to "trickle in" the plus efforts you commenced last year.

If you went after possibilities that could create new beginnings in business, new contacts and more modern, updated ways of bettering your finances and career, you'll see the results start to emerge at this time.

There could be job offers you never dreamed would come your way. Chance wears the robes of Lady Luck! Be receptive to all surprising new things coming your way. You deserve them.

You could form a partnership or create a team effort. Either will work well. You'll learn how to understand the advantages of working in groups. It's wise to be open to anything unusual this year. Accept the probability that a person of note, someone with excellent success in business, can show you certain tactical maneuvers that will aid you. Being flexible in a number 2 Personal Year is more important than being creative.

FRIENDSHIP AND FAMILY

Be alert to the reblossoming of old friendships. They've grown and you have changed. The past is forgotten. It's time to reap the rewards of the *now*. It's remarkable that you will discover the fun and joy you missed not seeing old buddies for the past several years. There are so many different things happening in their lives for you to be concerned or joyful about. There's always the sharing of great memories. As you met so many people in your number 1 Personal Year, all the fine plans you laid then will pop up unexpectedly at this time. The places you visited, faces you saw are of stimulating interest during your hours of relaxation this year. You won't have to work so hard either to garner the pleasure friendships bring.

Someday, when you are much older, and desire greatly to be around the circle of your young family, you will really understand what we're about to suggest. This year strive to "be there" when older relatives, parents, or others in their golden years contact you for companionship. If you're open, as you should be, the wisdom you hear and stories told you by elderly family members will leave its mark on your life and at the same time bring them the pleasure of your company.

ROMANCE AND LOVE

Nothing really good just "falls out of the sky" into your lap! But, slowly and surely you continue to realize you can and are commencing to renew the warm and loving marriage you once had. Attention to the small daily matters of living, the "please" and "thank you," is bringing more respect. Exhibiting your warmth and affection will increase the wonders of love in your life. So, too, in a number 2 Personal Year you come to full realization that all that you wanted isn't going to magically happen with your love object. Sit back, don't push, get angry, or squabble. You need more time and laid back effort. This year can be a boon in your life if you take your time. Be "second fiddle," if you're not talking, you'll be open to listening. Listen carefully, there's time at a later date to end affairs if it is what you must do. There should be no upheavals this year in your romantic life. Wait and be patient. All works out to your best interest sooner than you think.

HEALTH

Perhaps there's a nagging concern about a pain in your shoulder or a sore on your toe. Take the time to have a physician look at it. There will be no really serious problems you cannot handle at this time.

Your own forgetfulness to take prescribed medication or following instructions to aid healing is the only stumbling block. Be good to yourself and do what you must to maintain your vigor and excellent outlook on life.

Under the aspects of your health in a number 2 Personal Year, it is advisable you be reminded to just be yourself! You do not have to perform for anyone. When the tendency occurs to "act out" too often, you find yourself imitating others. You do not have to do this. If you allow your destiny to flow, you *are what you are supposed to be*. It means developing more of the good in you and overcoming that inclination to be less than you are.

GUIDELINES

Pettiness can become a big problem in a number 2 Personal Year. Be broad minded and overlook being childish in your actions; especially when you hear unflattering comments second hand. Being gullible and jumping to conclusions is not timely.

It can be a wonderful year in your life if you relax and watch the various trends of excellence come your way.

NUMBER 3 PERSONAL YEAR

FINANCES AND CAREER

No matter what your occupation, whether it is just satisfactory or very fulfilling, you may be drawn to boredom very easily this year. It's not exactly what you're doing to earn your bread, it's you and your desire to be free of all responsibility and have fun.

There's nothing wrong with flowing in a social environment more fully in a number 3 Personal Year. While at your work, make lunch a social event. Instead of grabbing a bite, lunch out in some interesting place with a co-worker, or friends. Be lively and enjoy the break from your daily routine. Dine at an ethnic restaurant. Call that old pal and meet for "catching up" on each others' present circumstances. It's even okay to lunch with some of your friends of the opposite sex. They'll understand your need to smile, laugh, and be affable during a work day. Project your personality. If you wish, tell jokes and make others laugh, then you can really feel "on stage."

Also, you have the opportunity this year to explore other avenues of productivity. If you choose to be before the public in your daily occupation, it may be worthwhile to make interview appointments after work to check into TV, radio, or public relations positions. This has been lingering in the back of your mind for some time. It's excellent timing to check out diverse opportunities. What better thing can you do but enhance your life with a fascinating career change? If that's really what you want, try it. See what happens.

FRIENDSHIP AND FAMILY

The sparkle in your life is not gone. Perhaps you've been allowing yourself to think that way because "nothing fun" is happening.

Your state of mind is controlled by no one else but you. It's up to you to be with family and friends. Have fun. Enjoy your blood ties with weekend excursions to parks and points of interest. See your parents, relatives, or siblings and enjoy parties you create. Arrange card games that invoke simple competition with a fairly small pot for the winner.

Friendship gets a boost this year. Don't play favorites. See all the people you enjoy. It's time for sing-alongs, karaoke, and western dancing. You don't have to be an accomplished professional to spend an evening or weekend joining in fun and games.

Take a few dancing lessons to learn disco! It's still a great way to let go.

ROMANCE AND LOVE

The year promises intimacy with the opposite sex. A person who can bring joy to your romantic life. You are particularly radiant this year; even blind dates could turn into that "forever" relationship you crave. Go for it. Allow the charisma each one of us has to come to the surface. You'll attract others you need for affection and maybe love. You have the ability this year to show your spouse how deeply you care. Don't be judgmental about his or her shortcomings. Show a cheerful face with an "up," spontaneous attitude. We allow love relationships to slip into habit, and taking each other for granted, break that pattern. Be the fun-loving social butterfly you would like to be.

HEALTH

Physical health in a number 3 Personal Year is usually vibrant. The tendency to slip and suffer the pain of disappointment and loss can create problems. Talk to yourself. Prevent excesses of alcohol consumption so your outlook will remain optimistic. Accept the assurance that you can create happiness in your life; it isn't all sorrow! Your health will be good and you'll feel strong by taking a stubborn attitude that all is well and will remain so if your outlook is bright. Take time to re-do your makeup to manufacture a more attractive "you." Or spend those extra dollars for a male model-look hair style. It's a good investment and aids in better mental health.

GUIDELINES

If your regular style is overly boisterous and people just don't approve, learn discrimination. Get to know the differences between worthy diversions and unprofitable blatant conduct.

Make it happen. Cultivate a happy disposition and avoid overspending. It isn't just money that brings the good life. It's your approach and ability to see the time is right to enjoy.

NUMBER 4 PERSONAL YEAR

FINANCES AND CAREER

This year could be one of the most decisive in your nine-year cycle. It's important to realize that a number 4 Personal Year is one that is potent with profitable methods of increasing your business. It also has educational opportunities to allow you the wonderful chance of adding to the knowledge you currently have to go forward.

Economically, it may not be that rewarding. But as all things go, time is required to devote oneself to learning and enhancing the framework or foundation of one's business abilities.

You will have cosmic forces to aid you in discovering why your career seems to be at a standstill. Maybe there are ways to help your work in a more substantial fashion. In the past, hit-or-miss schemes worked. Not this year. There are practical ways if you are open to learn and observe. See exactly how the product you are selling or the job you have can be better packaged or manipulated to bring more income.

Those of you involved in the sweeping technology of our time must understand you must *not* stand still. There are more sophisticated ways to accomplish your technical tasks. It's important you devote your time to learning new methods, short cuts or taking cues from your co-workers to improve your skills. Seminars or a ''how-to'' book can be a great advantage.

A co-worker may be absent due to illness or family problems. Their work may fall on your shoulders. If you accept this additional responsibility without a grudge, you'll find your time will be well spent. The added work could bring overtime in your paycheck.

FRIENDSHIP AND FAMILY

Unexpected events in family life seem to occur when demands at your work are likely to be burdensome. You can handle it. Once again, you may be called upon to do your chores at home as well as those of your spouse, roommate, or friend. Although you are well, it can be that sickness surrounds you. Little or large emergencies occur, demanding more of your time and effort. To fulfill yourself as a loving and compassionate friend or family member, expect this to happen and you'll be prepared to ''be there'' when others need you.

ROMANCE AND LOVE

This area of your life, at least the "romance" part, may be on hold for much of the year. When you are inundated by extra responsibility or spending too much time fulfilling your place as a family member, the essence of romance could be overlooked.

Love is there! You exhibit it by your concern and adapting to the needs of others. Looking for that special satisfaction of being the prince or princess in love is not prevalent at this time. Giving, caring, doing whatever you can to help is the key. If you do not "expect" passion you will not be disappointed. You can expect appreciation and gratefulness when you give without begrudging your time or effort.

HEALTH

To stay well yourself, you must get enough rest and keep your personal schedule uncluttered. There will be other times to be exceptionally busy for fun and hobbies.

This is an excellent year for stressing your substantial ability to perform in difficult work schedules, to learn new methods, and to aid yourself and others for future success in meeting your goals.

GUIDELINES

You must persevere in this year of demand. Training yourself not to falter is so very important.

It is not the time to leave your place of employment. Stay at this time. A change of positions could bring dire results. The flow is not with you now for change. Be determined to stick with it regardless of your emotional harness.

Use the discipline you may not have known you had and

arrange all you have to do on a realistic time table. Try as never before to be orderly and systematic and you'll come through with flying colors.

NUMBER 5 PERSONAL YEAR

FINANCES AND CAREER

A number 5 Personal Year is like a revolving door. You're in, you turn, you're out! It keeps moving your life in many different directions giving you momentary delight; all is well! Suddenly, changes occur beyond your control and everything that seemed A-OK no longer is!

Your activities at work may bring the illusion of ending. A while later, your job seems secure and you're certain all will work out very well. For sure, don't leave to take on another position. The timing is off. It's as if the fields only seem greener elsewhere. If you go, it doesn't work out.

Keep your eyes open and stay alert for unexpected changes. Many times some unforeseen event carries you forward in your next personal year that will be the perfect surrounding and bring the income you desire.

The future is very uncertain in a number 5 Personal Year. Pivotal changes could be upsetting. Try to remain calm and poised. Try to remember nothing in a number 5 Year remains permanent.

It's not a year to go into your own business. Anything new at this time does not fare well.

FRIENDSHIP AND FAMILY

Maintain this important part of your life in a simplistic way. If you are extremely tense due to the ongoing changes in your life, family and friends will take the brunt of it. You could be short-tempered and sharp-tongued; be careful of this tendency. Keep your equilibrium and keep your friends.

ROMANCE AND LOVE

Someone new could come into your life and sweep you off your feet. Like a thunderstorm, big noise, big excitement, then heavy rain—it's over. Childish tantrums could create friction in a love affair. Even misunderstandings don't last. Soon thereafter all will change again and you will be reconciled.

The urge to experiment sexually to check out new thrills is an exposure you don't need. More often than not you will feel abused by such a relationship and that kind of an adventure becomes a nightmare and a lost cause.

HEALTH

It is well to be extremely wary concerning your health. Symptoms may occur that seem quite serious, and may cause you and your family great concern. Usually it turns out to be very unimportant and should not be taken to heart. Most illnesses are caused by stress and if your nature is such that adjusting to this seemingly crazy year just isn't possible, pains will commence. You may sometimes feel the tension between your shoulders or in your lower back. Keep your tension in check. A humorous movie or comedic show will keep you laughing. Laughter aids most ills.

GUIDELINES

Forget those "feelings" you have and ignore indulging your *senses*. You have to use common *sense* to keep life on a more stable basis. Allow the freedom due you to alleviate the restlessness you feel. Particularly, don't nag. Allow others in your life the freedom due them. Your impatience will slowly dissipate as the year comes to a close.

NUMBER 6 PERSONAL YEAR

FINANCES AND CAREER

Although the main issues this year circulate about your home and love life, there are business matters that will also require your attention in a number 6 Personal Year.

There is every possibility you may be signing contracts concerning your occupation. It's important to remember that all agreements should be in writing. Verbal promises are unacceptable, for in the flow of this year, people will make promises they cannot keep. Believe only that which is reduced to writing.

If you had a problem with an associate or a partner, the vibrations are with you to work things out. Remain calm, cast no aspersions on their honesty or methods of doing business. At the same time, hold nothing back. You must be quite specific when laying out your point of view over anything that has been bothering you.

During this period you might decide to form an association with another person. Be sure you have a similar basic agreement with him or her on how things should be done. It will be either a partner or an associate who deals with such details as an administrator or accounting person. The vibrations at this time are with you and your choice will be correct.

If you feel an obsessive desire to decorate your office to create a more "you" look, do so! Just watch that you do not spend too much money. The office or place you work, your car, a warehouse, or manufacturing plant can be fixed up with some personal belongings to make it more homey.

Human relations "star" this year, not only in your personal life but in business as well. If there are any bridges to be mended with workers, do it this year. You'll win.

FRIENDSHIP AND FAMILY

There's a lot of conversation in your family life about making a move. In fact, it's been a matter of discussion for a few years. This cycle draws your decision to a head. You'll either be moving to a new residence or redecorating your home. This will occur whether you are living in a room, a larger apartment, or a house. Real estate values will be excellent to buy, if you can handle it this year.

You're operating on an even keel and can make good deals this year without floundering, without wondering if you're doing the right thing or not.

ROMANCE AND LOVE

Waiting in the wings is your next husband or wife. A new mate or lover comes into your life at this time and if your current relationship with your spouse or lover just isn't working out, this year you have an opportunity to change your life.

A monumental change of this sort is not easy. You may find yourself alone for some time. Many of you, whether or not you're happy and content in your current relationship, find fear prickling your spine. If there is a shadow of a doubt in your mind, do nothing. Your destiny will carry you into making the proper decisions when the time is right.

HEALTH

There will be a tendency to feel negative about your current situation in your home life. You must avoid a negative attitude, it could be mentally defeating. Continue to function properly in this year of change by looking at the bright side of your destiny.

There is even a possibility you may be feeling superior

to others; you may display an unpleasant show of self-righteousness and smugness. Why you are this way is easy to understand. In a number 6 Personal Year when all areas of your life are going well, one sometimes has to create problems when there are none.

GUIDELINES

Make cheerful and wise adjustments in your life. The vibrations of this year are with you.

NUMBER 7 PERSONAL YEAR

FINANCES AND CAREER

Professors at universities, teachers, many people with a philosophical bent to their personalities take a sabbatical in a number 7 Personal Year.

It's a time of removal from daily routines and, as Shakespeare said, "the slings and arrows of outrageous fortune."

Your need to be alone but not lonely is prevalent in a number 7 Personal Year. Travel away from your work or business sometime this year for a quiet vacation where nature is your entire environment, instead of glitzy hotel accommodations or fancy tours demanding association with groups of noisy merrymakers.

In life, there's always a lingering question about your occupation. "Is it really what I want?" "Do I find fulfillment in my work?" We are all so busy during the year we lose sight of the fact that we *can* answer our own questions.

Introspection about your work or career is in the *now*. Using self-analysis, you can begin correcting mistakes of the past and figuring ways to more aptly exploit your abilities to earn more money.

Even a sticky problem with your current work, that before you couldn't quite pin down, comes to the forefront of your mind; you now know what is wrong and how to correct it.

FRIENDSHIP AND FAMILY

The vacation or weekend excursions you take this year can include another who has the same spiritual values as you, one who sees that there must be moments of removal from the hubbub of life without dancing and playing. Those marvelous moments renew your faith in loved ones within your being by quietly acknowledging that life has been good to you.

ROMANCE AND LOVE

If you are unattached in a number 7 Personal Year, a very surprising and unexpected romantic meeting could occur while you're away from home base "cleansing your soul." Quite often relationships that happen accidentally during a number 7 Personal Year bring great peace into your life. They may also bring a better understanding of the importance of a new spiritual awakening.

A relationship established in a number 7 Personal Year may harbor some problems created by a third person. You must realize that this stumbling block may work itself out. Until the time that does happen, clandestine meetings may be necessary. Whatever the outcome, temporary or lasting, the gain you have is incomparable. You see the importance of having a person in your life with a marvelous spirit. It aids in making decisions about where you are and whether you should remain in your current love relationship.

HEALTH

We are all aware of the fact that physical and mental health are of the utmost importance. Sometimes we forget the spiritual health of our beings.

We begin to interpret our own actions. Are we too greedy? Is our lust overcoming good judgment? Do we spend enough "quality time" with our family, loved ones, or our children?

It is during this year answers to those questions become apparent. If we desire a healthy spiritual attitude, we will listen carefully to our own answers and by our own decisions do what's right.

GUIDELINES

We have an unusual chance in a number 7 Personal Year to find we are the recipients of unexpected monies. Inheritances, out of court settlements, and income from surprising sources bring us unexpected funds.

The apparent negative aspects of this year are easily recognizable. Don't flog yourself for past mistakes. Accept those facts and go forward with a vow not to let it happen again.

If you have been hurt in the near past and this realization comes to you, do not carry revenge in your being; forgive and forget.

Stick to the realities of life. Admit there are peaks and valleys for everyone, including yourself. Dwell on the best ways to enrich your soul and share with others of the same mind.

NUMBER 8 PERSONAL YEAR

FINANCES AND CAREER

This year is a milestone in your life, one you will cherish in the future as one of the momentous periods of your current nine-year Life Cycle.

Your economic status dynamically changes for the better if you handle the 8 Number Vibration of this year correctly.

Branch out! Whatever your occupation, press to make it larger, more active, more income. Have great faith in yourself. You can do it. The power of concentration is the basis of your success in this potent year.

Not only hard work brings results but sincerity in your efforts along with good common sense. Specifically follow through on projects you start.

Being an idealist, forget the attitude that money is not one of your greatest needs. One thing to remember, reach high in every desire you have. Go to the top man or woman who can help you. Don't settle for the lieutenants or foot soldiers. Be aware, alert and ready to go after big opportunities.

FRIENDSHIP AND FAMILY

This year will reward you. There will be justice. In your work, planning and efforts, you will find the success you're after. Allow family to do favors for you. There should be no thought of "payback," just, "Thanks for what you are doing for me."

ROMANCE AND LOVE

The social side of life must be fit in properly so there's a balance to your achievement. Work is to be rewarded with pleasure. Especially romance. You can rekindle lost ardor with a lover. And if you are searching for a new person to share your life, don't be afraid to go after the fulfillment of security as well as love in this new challenge. Money and protective love for either sex can make a coupling much more comfortable.

HEALTH

Each step you take will be a turning point on the way. Don't allow yourself to falter. Keep the energy in your mind and the body will respond to the momentum of your thoughts. Do not cease going after your economic rewards.

GUIDELINES

To avoid pitfalls of this year's aggressive attitude you must fend off all deep-rooted fears of ending up in poverty. It's all up to you. Your attitude toward success and your acceptance of the fact that you are going to "make it" will help.

It's time you became somewhat relentless in your efforts to go up. The humanistic, charitable attitudes you have must be submerged slightly for now. *You* are the project! Work diligently at it.

NUMBER 9 PERSONAL YEAR

FINANCES AND CAREER

This is it! The end of your nine-year Cycle. If it has been good, you've done all you can to allow your life to go forward into the blue sky beyond and out of any storms still trailing from the past.

You'll be moving fast. Eliminating everything and everybody in your business environment who have been "hangers on," relentlessly using up your energy and demanding your attention. Let it all go. Remove those papers you've been saving forever, feeling, "I'll use them some day!" You won't! What has been useless through the last life cycle has less and less meaning in a number 9 Personal Year.

Now is the time to bring the loose ends of your job together. To stay or go? Is it good for you? Is it just a convenience that has no room for growth? You have the answers to these questions, this is the time. Unload *now* and let your life go forward.

This year let the top people at your office know who and what you are. If you deserve more, don't hesitate to blow your own horn. Don't slip into being afraid of the future. Exclaim your successes and let all know of your accomplishments.

Make a list of all you wish to maintain at work as well as an inventory of what you want from here on. All cosmic forces are on your side. Take advantage of the furious storm of change surrounding you.

FRIENDSHIP AND FAMILY

The ongoing drain of money you constantly give to so-called friends must cease. Your relationships with them are not adding to your stature as a progressing person. Your giving them funds whenever they are "short" is really not helping them to fulfill their own potential. On rare occasions all of us could find ourselves in this position. When it becomes a constant drain, you must cease. *Unload.* That's the word which should be the most significant one you think and use during this number 9 Personal Year.

Use that extra money to "see the world." Share vacations with loved ones who were witness to your funding these "friends." Appreciation is not only what they'll feel but will be sincerely happy for you that you realized your errors.

ROMANCE AND LOVE

For varied reasons, many of them inexplicable to ourselves, we let love affairs go on that are truly over. We're fearful of not replacing that *habit* that's bad for us. Better to end a bad habit and have none at all and allow ourselves to grow properly with a healthy, positive romantic involvement.

We kid ourselves by saying to ourselves like a mantra, "What will the children do in a one-parent household?" What will they do? They'll adjust. Being witness to a marriage where only one partner gives is certainly not a healthy situation for them to observe. It takes great strength to end a situation where children are involved. Maybe you can change and adapt to what your mate feels you should be. You're the only and best judge of that. Remember, you cannot change anyone else! You can only change yourself.

HEALTH

The essence of elimination is prominent as well in a number 9 Personal Year in the physical sense of the word.

If you've been putting off minor surgery, getting your eyes examined or your teeth attended to, this year is the time. Don't put off those "body" items that require attention. Commence doing something about it this year.

If lack of exercise has been a bone in your throat, start now. Do a few exercises at first, and slowly, add more thereafter. Anything which you've put off concerning more vibrant health should be attended to now. If vitamins have been approved by your physician, take them. Are you afraid to feel better? It is not unusual for you to procrastinate. When you know the time is right, which is in a number 9 Personal Year, there are no more excuses for delay.

GUIDELINES

You could defeat the fine aspects of this year by being wasteful of your energy and money. Draw an outline exactly as you wish to go. Don't scatter your forces all over the place by lack of concentration. Emerge from this number 9 Personal Year with another more secure goal in mind. You'll make it!

CHAPTER NINE

How to Calculate Your Personal Month.

THERE ARE NINE MONTHS IN EVERY PERSONAL
YEAR. AFTER YOU UNDERSTAND HOW TO
CALCULATE YOUR PERSONAL MONTH, YOU WILL
FIND THEY ARE HIGHLIGHTED WITH INFORMATION
TO CARRY YOU THROUGH TO A FULL NINE MONTHS
OF THE COUNT IN NUMEROLOGY.

After you have determined what your Personal Year is,
add it to each month of the year. For example: If you are
in a Number 7 Personal Year and you wish to know what
Personal Month you are in during January through December, do the following:

January,	1 Month: 7+1=8. January is your Personal Month number 8.
February,	2 Month: 7+2=9. February is your Personal Month number 9.
March,	3 Month: 7+3=10. 1+0=1. March is your Personal Month number 1. Always reduce a double digit down to one number.
April,	4 Month: 7+4=11. 1+1=2. April is your Personal Month number 2.
May,	5 Month: 7+5=12. 1+2=3. May is your Personal Month number 3.

June,   6 Month: 7+6=13. 1+3=4. June is your
                          Personal Month number 4.

July,   7 Month: 7+7=14. 1+4=5. July is your
                          Personal Month number 5.

August,   8 Month: 7+8=15. 1+5=6. August is your
                          Personal Month number 6.

September,   9 Month: 7+9=16. 1+6=7. September is
                          your Personal Month
                          number 7.

October,   10 Month: 7+10=17. 1+7=8. October is
                          your Personal Month
                          number 8.

November, 11 Month: 7+11=18. 1+8=9. November is
                          your Personal Month
                          Number 9.

December, 12 Month: 7+12=19. 1+9=10. 1+0=1.
                          December is your Personal
                          Month number 1.

At the beginning of the book there is a description and answer to "What is Numerology?" By being aware of your Personal Year and particularly your Personal Month you can see clearly whether it's time to reap a harvest, sit back and watch the world go by, or study. There could be help from the cosmos to aid you. It surrounds you. It will help in your learning process.

Knowing all of the above brings better understanding, heightened anticipation, and less disappointment if things are just not going your way.

As discussed earlier, Pythagorean Numerology works in a Nine-Year Cycle. After number 9 Personal Month, in February (if you are in a number 7 Personal Year as shown in the example), you re-enter a number 1 Personal Month in March.

NUMBER 1 MONTH

This month gives you another chance at winning what you desire. You feel cheerful and sure about yourself. Offers and people who are new to you bring great hope for the balance of the year. New contacts should be nurtured. You can always let go of those that do not measure up to your standards. You cannot know unless you try. There could be travel this month to check out a new possibility for your work or fun. Take advantage of any short trips.

NUMBER 2 MONTH

In this hectic year you must make enough time to relax. This month is perfect. Relax but stay alert to the varied opportunities that may be presented to you. There are some minor problems, but none so great that you cannot handle them with common sense and patience.

Rekindle old acquaintances. Reaffirm friendships by exhibiting your concern and desire to help. In turn, you'll find these very people will be determined to aid you in simple but important ways.

Since you will find the time to rest this month, recharge your batteries by attending stimulating events where you are the observer, not a participant.

It is best at this time to use self discipline and do not allow yourself to slip into thinking gloomy thoughts. It could lead to a depression. You don't deserve to do that to yourself. Playing second-fiddle does not last for long. Toward the end of this month you'll feel the fun comin'.

NUMBER 3 MONTH

Special treats await you. It's frolic time socially. Special functions like family gatherings or parties where you can shine are very fulfilling.

Invitations come your way. Attend these unique affairs; tours of historical houses, trips to arboretums, fashion shows. Project your personality and enjoy yourself. Feeling very frivolous, there might be a tendency to overspend. Keep the drawstrings on your purse tighter than usual. The gaiety you feel is due you. Enjoy all things coming your way.

NUMBER 4 MONTH

As the world turns so does the winding path of life. The nooks and crannies of the path you are walking requires attention to details. Apply that fine mind you have to the tasks you've been putting off.

Adjust your budget, do justice to the projects that you've started and left unfinished. Your pets require grooming for their comfort, not just their beauty. If you've been planning to polish or paint your favorite furniture, get the proper wax and paint to do the job. Your efforts to repair household items will encourage the lazy person you've felt like to become the enthusiastic person you are.

An appointment with your physician for a check-up is warranted. Not because you're not feeling well but to make certain your health remains in tip-top condition.

NUMBER 5 MONTH

Destiny and the fine fabric of the tapestry of life becomes more muddled. You expect one thing to happen and just like a hurricane something else is tossed in your lap. The word *disappointment* should be removed from your vocabulary. Life plays like a country fiddle, happy and dancing one day, low-down and burdensome the next. Try to remember that there's very little that remains permanent at this time. It's a taste of this, a bit of that. If your emotions are particularly topsy-turvy this month, don't be alarmed. Any decision in romantic areas of life will not be permanent. Whatever occurs will be resolved within twenty-five days. Just flow with the rhythm of this unexpectedly wind-blown month.

There you are in deep thought observing the tapestry of your life in this month of constant change. The colors you see, you are sure, are green and lilac. You go closer and it changes to blue! You think, ah, that's a picture of my parents when they were very young, you turn your head and it's not them at all, but it's you when you were a little child. The days and hours and moments keep changing like a kaleidoscope. With these ongoing transformations and illusions you could become extremely confused, not understanding why life is so unsure. Don't philosophize. Just go with the tide and enjoy the variety of tidbits offered.

NUMBER 6 MONTH

A month of beauty, adjustment, and choice to change the surroundings in your home. Perhaps the addition of a new china or chess set. Maybe it's different colored walls in your kitchen or new plants to nourish with care and attention. All this adds to the loveliness of your environment. You might decide to make a move to a different apartment or home. Perhaps a decision now to renew old acquaintances that could evolve into romance is timely. Or maybe the time has come to end a love affair that's brought only frustration and unhappiness. Your timing is excellent to end all areas of agitation. Family is highlighted. Cousins, nephews, or old friends you've neglected for no reason—resume these relationships, it will bring you pleasant days and lovely evenings.

Partners or associates in business require some of your caring attention, too. If you choose to shrug off responsibilities your judgement is incorrect. Spend time with others now sharing mutual cultural interests. Develop more in your hobbies or avocation. Add to that fund of knowledge that brings joy into your life.

NUMBER 7 MONTH

If all year seemed to be an ongoing trial of learning, "things" to be done and not enough time to do them, this month is your answer to true receptivity and passiveness.

Aggression fails. Sit back and evaluate yourself. Take an inventory of where you are in life. Has where you are and what you've done brought favorable results? Are you thankful for the feelings of peace that permeate your spirit? Self-analysis is the means by which you'll get your answers. Psychically, your feelings will not delude you. If you are quiet and you listen carefully to that inner voice, the elements of your existence will bear fruit. Impatience, suspicion of people you love, or resentment will only perplex you. A quiet spirit and more simple diet than usual will bring the rewards you seek without fanfare. It's a time of spiritual awareness; travel to places you've never seen for nature's sake.

NUMBER 8 MONTH

This month will test what you're working at so diligently. Practical matters such as balancing your checkbook and budgets should be attended to. Arrange business meetings to alert your partners, friends, or family that you really mean what you're about. Get down to basics. Find ways to increase your income by selling items of worth that have no meaning to you. Get your music, poetry, or book to an agent. You may be successful having it published. Take a chance. Win or lose, you're trying. Check out the investment plans provided by the company you work for, or commence saving money, somehow, some way, even fifty dollars per month. It grows! Take the initiative concerning your own financial future.

Forget about worrying where you'll find funds to survive. It can be as simple as babysitting or finding a few extra hours at a phone answering service. You could lose the complete perfection of this month by spending foolishly or totally ignoring all the cosmic values going your way to aid you economically. It's a month that alerts you to making good deals, whatever they may be.

NUMBER 9 MONTH

Be wary of loss. It's a combined effort by the vibrations this month to help in letting go of the people, papers, pictures in your life that you no longer need. Along with this, watch out for the loss of money, keys, pieces of clothing that are meaningful to you, keepsakes, or objects that bring you pleasure.

Your temperament may not be as tranquil as you wish to keep peace with someone you love. Avoid unimportant arguments. Chaos you create may lose you a good friend. Keep an impersonal attitude when confronted with others' peculiarities. No one is perfect. It's your choice to ignore thoughtless acts; this would be the month to wear blinders to all emotional scenes. Like the three monkeys, see nothing, hear nothing, say nothing. Just go on your way discarding all that has lost the importance or meaning it once had.

CHAPTER TEN

Chaldean Numerology:
The Mysterious and Curious Meaning of Your
Double Number Vibration.

THIS SIMPLE TASK WILL GIVE YOU TRUE INSIGHT
INTO THE BASIC YOU. CHALDEAN NUMEROLOGY IS
MYSTERIOUS, BUT ALLOWS AND EXPLAINS THE
MANY DIMENSIONS OF SELF.

Occult, as defined in the dictionary, reads, "involving
the supernatural; mystical, magical" or "beyond the range
of ordinary knowledge." There are other meanings listed
but experience proves that Chaldean Numerology seems to
find explicitly those personality traits of an individual that
are unseen, unknown to the casual observer. Sometimes,
even the person whose Chaldean Numbers are explained is
just beginning to fathom the meaning of the many unexpected avenues of self. They are making a new discovery
of the subtle areas of their being that before came in
glimpses. Now, clearly, the double numbers or two-digit
meanings will openly express the hidden influences revealed in a name. There is, too, a prognostication fore-
shadowing the individual's destiny.

This portion will perhaps bring to you some very unexpected and important information.

Somehow, as all mysteries require solutions, only you
will be able to solve the sometimes perplexing questions
manifested in your own Chaldean Numerology vibrations!

The following chart is easy to decipher. The first line of

the chart shows the numbers 1 through 8. Under the digit 1 are the letters *A, I, J, Q,* and *Y.* If any of the letters in your name are those indicated above they carry the number value of one.

Under the digit 2 are the letters *B, K,* and *R.* If any letters in your name are those indicated they carry the number value of two.

Under the digit 3 are the letters *C, G, L,* and *S.* If any of the letters in your name are those indicated they carry the number value of three.

Under the digit 4 are the letters *D, M,* and *T.* If any of the letters in your name are those indicated they carry the number value of four.

Under the digit 5 are the letters *E, H, N,* and *X.* If any of the letters in your name are those indicated they carry the number value of five.

Under the digit 6 are the letters *U, V,* and *W.* If any of the letters in your name are those indicated they carry the number value of six.

Under the digit 7 are the letters *O* and *Z.* If any of the letters in your name are those indicated they carry the number value of seven.

Under the digit 8 are the letters *F* and *P.* If any of the letters in your name are those indicated they carry the number value of eight.

Therefore, if your name is Sally, S = 3, A = 1, L = 3, L = 3, and Y = 1. SALLY = 3 + 1 + 3 + 3 + 1 = 11. As you read on you will see what the number value of eleven means. You will do the exact same thing with your last name.

We believe this will give you a clear picture of how to calculate any name. Following are more examples of Chaldean Name calculations for your clarification.

Enjoy the adventure!

In Chaldean Numerology *you must use double numbers.* In other words, you *do not* reduce numbers to a single digit.

On occasion, an individual's name may be a single letter. In that event, the Chaldean would be a Number 1–9. By using the chart below, you will be able to determine and calculate correctly, the Chaldean Number values of the letters in your Current Name Used.

1	2	3	4	5	6	7	8
A	B	C	D	E	U	O	F
I	K	G	M	H	V	Z	P
J	R	L	T	N	W		
Q		S		X			
Y							

W A L T   D I S N E Y
6+1+3+4 4+1+3+5+5+1
14   + 19
Total name = 33

A L I N A   Q U I N T A N A
1+3+1+5+1 1+6+1+5+4+1+5+1
11   +   24
Total name = 35

B I L L   C L I N T O N
2+1+3+3 3+3+1+5+4+7+5
9   +   28
Total name = 37

BIRTH CERTIFICATE NAME

If you desire, you can also calculate the Chaldean Number Value of letters in your name on your birth certificate then compare them with your Current Name Used. You will be amazed at a few startling differences and as well surprised that no matter how your name changes for whatever reason, the thread of meaning runs similarly through all.

NUMBER 1 CHALDEAN

You insist on getting your way. There is no dealing with you when you're on this roller-coaster. There is no compromise. You seem to adapt to a rise and fall in ventures. You go too high, but even if you hit bottom, you can handle it. There's an inbred power with a number 1 vibration and you use this power wisely.

Since you usually lead the pack you've learned you do have the facility to guide others.

Your energies should be harnessed and focused on the goal. An internal force emanates through all actions and endeavors. It's not unusual for you to be successful at all times.

Be aware to follow your heart and regardless of what people say, employ your efforts to do the greatest good for the greatest number of people.

You're similar to a skyrocket shooting high in the sky. Then another and another! With every rocket that fizzles out, you know that with an ending there is always a new beginning.

Be patient, especially with yourself, and others will continue to follow and win with you as their leader.

NUMBER 2 CHALDEAN

An immense fireball of activity surrounds you. Taking it apart bit by bit brings no joy. You do not have to analyze, just enjoy. You could defeat the wondrous excitement you stir up. Let the fireballs dance crazily in your life and have some fun.

It's a joke when you lose your temper! Talk about tact and discretion! You don't know the meaning of the words. Hey, let it out. All things pass, and some people deserve your anger; they cannot handle the truth. Truth, to them, is a bare, unshaded lightbulb shining in their eyes. It smarts and burns.

If you make a promise, keep it or don't make it. Just use that "special something" you have, like calling if you're going to be late. Patience is its own reward; watch and see that this is correct. Having too wide a range of curiosity can keep you stumbling. Finish one project before starting another. If you look for the "jokes" life plays, you'll be a merrier person. Why? Because you are truly alive, naturally honest, and you see the humor in the varied episodes constantly happening around you.

NUMBER 3 CHALDEAN

You have an excellent mental agility and a wonderful imagination. You can do anything you'd like to do. The object here is to stick to it. Follow through! This will bring your dreams into reality.

You were meant to be in some form of service to help others. The love you feel is limitless. You can set a fine example by following your inner nature to the best of your ability on a daily basis. Doing this will create a profound effect on all those around you.

You're good with figures, you have a fine touch with detail. You can do anything from punching out on a cash register to being a nuclear scientist.

Let go of situations and debris in your life that are no longer useful to you, especially suffocating relationships. Let go. Once you do, don't look back, even mentally.

The past is a canceled check, the present is here and now, and the future is a promissory note. Your best path will be in the here and now as you center on home base.

NUMBER 4 CHALDEAN

You feel a close fellowship with men and women. The power you have must be used wisely. If used negatively to put people in their place, it will kick back on you. Be kind.

There is a special door to enter or a private place within you where you go to meditate and think things out. The more time you spend in this "place," the more incredibly your life will flourish. You are naturally studious, pondering, and thoughtful. You can and do explore all possibilities. Let go of all grudges and forget about revenge. Clear the slate; forgive yourself first. If you maintain impeccability in each compartment of your life from the status of your thoughts through the continuity of basic living, your life will be rewarding.

Laugh more, see that fun and play are part of life. Enjoy being *joyful.*

Your mind is very strong and determined. Your heart is like the sun. Your mind cannot blank out the sun. Concentrate on letting the heart feel and express and letting the mind do its own thing. In you, they are separate and partitioned. For your own good do not play mind games with others to stretch your heart and mind too far out for anything not for their greatest good.

Be here now. You're a realist. Close your eyes and picture the color lavender often; try it every day for thirty-three days and see what happens.

NUMBER 5 CHALDEAN

You're fun! With your rakish sense of humor, laughter is your buffer to life. You don't live in the past but are constantly making comparisons between then and now; usually in a positive sense. You dislike being trapped by anyone or anything. Freedom is important for your happiness so you will be able to do all things you desire. For example; trying different occupations, meeting new people, pursuing adventure. This is exciting, rewarding, and fruitful.

Instinctively you see the real personality within people, but are not interested in trying to be like anyone else. Just be yourself and enjoy your helter-skelter activity. Do things in the moment, unpremeditated. You are "doing" life in the *now*. It is your nature to remain open to new ideas and to remain a student of life.

NUMBER 6 CHALDEAN

Again, you have that emptiness, no love. Your shyness while growing up had an indelible bearing on your adult life. Your selections of one or two friends were usually people who were considered underdogs. Those that were left out, rejected for one reason or another, became your companions.

An inherent love of music always brings you pleasure. Uplifting, lovely colors surround you. Creative hobbies you do by yourself are fun. You do not want to be what others feel you should be. You know yourself and must do what you feel is best to keep you happy.

There is a tendency to overindulgence for immediate gratification. If you keep yourself emotionally detached, your power lies in balance within. Life is like a slot machine, if you are "tilted," you could lose.

You have the innate ability to troubleshoot and see clearly how often others can be better; it's great you can recognize this and accept the reality of people as they are.

Peace and harmony are pivotal forces in your life. Anything that could distract this should be eliminated. It's taken you too long and you've worked too hard to blow it.

NUMBER 7 CHALDEAN

You enjoy fast movement, as if intuitively you are pressed for action. At times you're so changeable it's difficult to set yourself on a definite path. When you allow this confusion to upset you, nothing is accomplished. It's important that when you "know without knowing" what you have chosen to do is correct, do it!

You have a tendency to color the truth because you do not wish to hurt anyone's feelings, but you resent being deluded by others. You must investigate this negativity about yourself and try diligently to correct it. Most people will adjust to truth. If they don't, it's their problem, not yours.

Sometimes you have an uncontrollable temper, blasting off too soon. Curb this part of your nature. Develop the patience required before you *blow your stack!* You are basically a fair person and there's no need to create discomfort, especially around co-workers. You see beyond the moment and the words; *stupid, foolish,* and *unjust* are the words that ignite your short fuse.

NUMBER 8 CHALDEAN

This is the area in your numerological analysis that defines a person as having a fanatical spiritual drive. For example, a nun or priest or maybe a lay person in the church who is devoutly religious. There's nothing wrong with this, but is it you? You should be involved but not so deeply that life's pattern takes on the guise of a preacher.

This vibration, as strange as it may seem, also denotes an appreciation of money, an understanding of what it will do to aid in your life and how financial security is important to survival.

If just a little of these feelings described did not exist with you in earlier years of your life, you could find you must work hard on eliminating a greed and possessiveness that does not allow your spontaneity to shine through. The loneliness brought by concentrating on monetary accomplishments will disperse like a rain cloud when you make a deliberate attempt to end unworthy pressures. That dark cloud will cease to hover over your life.

You do feel that deep sense of knowing there is either a great force much larger and indefinable than yourself which is your inner voice. Or for you, it could be the wondrousness of nature that holds you captive and in awe.

NUMBER 9 CHALDEAN

You are a tireless fighter in all you attempt in life. Yours is a vibration of success through will, grit, and determination.

Your hasty temper and very impulsive needs make it quite clear about your desire to be your own person. Control must be exercised in this area or all your hard work is brought to a halt in life's endeavors.

Your very courageous being is real. It is the attitude of a leader and if you are involved in the military, you command with great judgment.

Again, impulsiveness in word and deed is self-defeating. In a state of semi-anger, due to your mind-set, you will be prone to accidents. Somehow fire and explosions accompany this death-defying vibration.

The strife caused by your belligerent actions badly effects family relationships. Watch it.

A resentment of criticism lies dormant under your cover of independence and self-confidence. Your short fuse is ready to ignite at the simplest disagreement.

Unless you are in full control, you are not interested. You

want not only responsibility but the complete authority to go with it!

There's an ongoing craving for affection and sympathy. In love affairs both men or women with this vibration must be aware that you can be easily manipulated. That is, until you catch on!

NUMBER 10 CHALDEAN

You insist on getting your way. There is no dealing with you when you're on this roller coaster. There is no compromise. You seem to adapt to a rise and fall in ventures. You go too high, but even if you hit bottom, you can handle it. There's an inbred power with a number 10 vibration and you use this power wisely.

Since you usually lead the pack, you've learned you do have the facility to guide others.

Your energies should be harnessed and focused on the goal. An internal force emanates through all actions and endeavors. It's not unusual for you to be successful at all times.

Be aware to follow your heart and regardless of what people say, employ your efforts to do the greatest good for the greatest number of people.

You're similar to a skyrocket shooting high in the sky. Then another and another! With every rocket that fizzles out, you know that with an ending there is always a new beginning.

Be patient, especially with yourself, and others will continue to follow and win with you as their leader.

NUMBER 11 CHALDEAN

Life has placed you as a witness in front of the grand jury, constantly being questioned and tested. Hardships attach themselves to you as if you were a magnet. But it is your inborn expertise to come out of these difficulties with much ease.

Your understanding is uncanny. This is why you listen to only those of the highest authority or accept input or information only from experts. Rather than "do" for others, there's a need to help people help themselves. You are attracted to the underdog and relish a challenge. You've learned not to allow the burdens of others to rub off on you.

Self-discipline from within is imperative. Your energies must be used for your own progress as opposed to giving so much help to others. Their approval is not required. You know you do the right thing.

You do best in a one-to-one relationship. It relieves you of taking yourself and problems around you so seriously. Try to detach from others' anguish; sit back, listen, and observe. See and understand what is consciously happening around you when others are in turmoil. Do this at all times.

Keep your perspective and know the wheel of life continually evolves just like the four seasons. Events do change. Let go and get in the flow.

NUMBER 12 CHALDEAN

If you feel as if you've been taken advantage of, been manipulated, or done things only to please others because you are expected to, that can change now if it hasn't already.

If you are aware of your own needs, there is a connection between being the victim and being the person *you* want to be: *be the person you want to be.* You're not a puppet on a string. You are a total vessel and can tap into yourself to be of service if you wish. Do it your way. Let the light flow through you and you will be nourished and others will, as well.

You could be an excellent counselor and owe it to yourself to try. Terrific revelations come when you do not allow yourself to be used.

You enjoy being helpful, but don't jump in too fast. Get a picture of what has to be done and do not permit yourself to be captured and placed in a cage. Watch this tendency on a day-to-day basis.

You have a fondness for travel and everywhere you go you have the ability to be like the people that live there. You see the reality. You see what you must for what it is and enjoy it in an unaffected way.

Stay in a frame of mind of gratitude and thankfulness. This will bring more.

NUMBER 13 CHALDEAN

Although your brusque manner doesn't show it, you have deep and sensitive feeling for humanity. You draw opposite-thinking people to compromise. It is a power that can be devastating if used unwisely. Be considerate at all times.

Your conscience is your master. Integrity drives you to analyze all problems. Within you, the ability to work out others' difficult situations is incredible. Every possible angle is fully seen. Continue in this manner. Truth is your threshold to freedom and allows a flowing continuity to your own life.

Sometimes you forget it's all right to joke, have a good time. Basically your mental prowess is the mainstay of your existence. Allow yourself to feel those pure wanderings of your heart. At times, yield to your emotions. You always seem to know when.

Being a realist, you live in the now. When you are particularly adamant about doing it your way, imagine a luscious screen in front of your closed eyes, painted in luxurious shades of pale pink to deep mauve. It will quiet your being and permit you to be the loving person you are.

NUMBER 14 CHALDEAN

You are capable of deep understanding of others and treasure your ability to love deeply. There is a plus and a minus here. Because you feel deeply, you are often hurt by lovers when you are too dependent on them. Rely on your own inner strength. Be aware of all that is around you. If you sense it's necessary to speak about your discontent, *do so*. Then, *let it go,* say it with a proper outburst of emotion, that clears the air. Only you control what you will allow to reach you. Anything that brings injustice or pain is not for you. Be self-reliant and you will not be disappointed when you believe what others say and they let you down. You have learned to decipher truth from untruth. The psychic part of your nature is a protective cloak.

Use your varied interests to further inner growth. Painting, reading, writing, working with your hands are all pleasantly rewarding and help you to settle confusion. These "tricks" work to manifest no carryover from previous difficult circumstances.

When you are argumentative, fight for those who are right. Deception is as inevitable as night following day. You're sure what you say is the truth, but do not trust others too readily. Wait to be sure you are not being deluded.

Laugh, these people really are deluding themselves.

NUMBER 15 CHALDEAN

You have a sincere interest in the occult and know you have a magnetism whereby people like to do things for you.

Your excellent speaking voice is perfect for the radio or other media, and on the telephone your voice serves you well. Even speaking before the public on any issues can be successful.

You say, "Why me?" It's a setup! You attract problems so you have to handle them. Sometimes the best way to *do* this is *not to!* Everything has its season.

Being in any situation where you need the approval of others is not good. Don't worry about hurting anyone, the truth sets you free. What you really desire is to be *free*.

You don't like the unexpected; you need your navigation charts intact so you know you have balance and a destination.

In a loving way be much more selfish with your time and self. Take care of your own needs. You've been out there too much for everybody but yourself.

NUMBER 16 CHALDEAN

You are the keeper of the keys. You can open doors to others' feelings. Keep listening for the voice within. Some call it intuition, inner guidance, knowing without knowing, or you may have no name for it at all. If it is a prevalent part of your life you must allow yourself to be guided by it.

Honesty is important. You can't plan too far in advance. With so many changes imminently taking place in your life, just jump in and follow the flow that guides you.

It's perfectly natural that there is a quiet side within you that few people are able to see. You are incredible at keeping secrets. Your greatest joy is in detaching from the craziness of the world.

Travel looks like a lot of fun. Your awareness and observation is uncanny. Be near water. It has a magical effect on you; from the ocean to the rain.

The unknown is known to you by what you see and feel. You can bypass explanations.

Life may appear to be a Ferris wheel with people occupying each seat. Stop going backwards or in reverse, that's what you have been doing. It's like trying to walk down a long escalator that is going up.

Spend time with nature in its simplest forms such as at parks and beaches. When new information comes through you, allow it to be expressed in writing or any other artistic outlet. Destiny and Fate hold you in loving arms.

NUMBER 17 CHALDEAN

Good, good, good! This is a beautiful vibration; open, sharing, action in a pure sense. The childlike quality within you is so wonderful and real. Let the beauty shine, uncontaminated by this world.

Instead of giving so much to everybody else, why not start giving and investing in *yourself?*

You cannot write checks to all who need help if your bank account is empty. Keep your tank full at all times, then share the abundance from your overflow. Be content where you are. Appreciate all that you have.

NUMBER 18 CHALDEAN

This is a difficult vibration. There is a powerful tendency to break away from family, unfold and design your own life your way.

When you cut the cord or sever yourself from loved ones, you are willing to go through a jungle and hack away the excessive foliage with a machete, to find your own way. This is the perfect method to see who you are and accepting yourself.

You are nonjudgmental and free of condemnation of yourself and others.

''I am what I am, I am what I am!'' That's the slogan of your life.

Due to your earlier rebelliousness, you are now a survivor and able to exist freely. The world is your home.

All the parts of the puzzle of ''you'' fit! It seems there were extra pieces that were not required and they will be eliminated. Automatically you will know that all is well.

NUMBER 19 CHALDEAN

You are like sunshine radiating its light to all those around you. You are music. You are guided with inner strength. Your kindness, compassion, and understanding is exquisite. You are quick and enjoy seeing people laughing around you. You are funny and fun to be with.

Think about this, which way is up? You are always in the *now* and open to life's multicolored changes.

You understand the cycles of life; nothing remains the same. What we have today is *now*.

Your commitment to life is magnificent!

NUMBER 20 CHALDEAN

The higher part of this vibration is being good to yourself in all of your actions.

If there is anything you do which is NOT good for you for whatever reason from the past, let it go. If you have negative feelings, see it, observe it, and understand it. Then be good to yourself. Do a one-eighty-degree turn and be the best you can for you.

There is a tendency for you to be influenced by your surroundings as you cannot tolerate mental or physical pain. Be the captain of your ship and keep yourself tuned through proper diet and exercise.

You are far from the word ordinary. You *are* different. Don't be one of the crowd; you do not have to go down to anyone else's level.

You see beauty in all forms and this is really seeing the beauty inside you. Stay focused on that. If thoughts or situations try to pull you back, let them pass. Soon you'll see the sunshine and rainbows.

It's important you feel comfortable. You are self-taught now and need to apply what you know to your garden in life. Be an example through your actions and do not be overinvolved in trying to change others. You have to do what you have to do, and so do others in their unfolding.

NUMBER 21 CHALDEAN

Inner truth. Patience. If things seem a long time coming, it is all part of the plan.

Out of a country pond grows a gorgeous water lily with its pads of lush green. You cannot compromise with inner truth. You know the difference.

You are honorable and everything you do is done with dignity.

Being out in the world, making people happy is your happiness. Your greatest joy is chasing gloom, aiding small children if they are handicapped, and bringing conversation and companionship to others' golden years.

Your sincerity and smiles are nourishment for the world to behold.

NUMBER 22 CHALDEAN

Either your body or mind is extremely active at all times. Exercise is an antidote to restlessness. Even tasks that require mechanical ability come easy to you although dealing with this particular attribute on a full-time basis would not bring you much happiness.

There is a tendency to hold back expressing physical and mental pain. You'd rather keep the anguish to yourself than explain to others what your problems are until you have the results of medical testing if it's physical. If it's a problem you're dealing with mentally, here again you must understand all the parameters of what's bothering you before you express your emotions.

You are impeccably neat and orderly without seeming to be a perfectionist. All must be in correct order when you're working at any project. The papers you handle provide a steady flow of information written and easy to read. Your follow-through is continually aided by careful notetaking and the sure progressive plans you make. It was a happy day when you started making lists.

To be sure you're on the right track as you progress through all the necessary steps to achieving your goal, your ability to master concepts is important. Those "lists" of things to be done are lifesavers.

NUMBER 23 CHALDEAN

You are able to do many things and have infinite interests at the same time.

Things you do tend to be magical. Doors open readily. Being a free spirit you allow others to blossom or fly.

Unpredictable as you are, try not wearing a watch for five days. You'll enjoy it.

You do best when unexpected events occur. You also have the ability to learn two or more languages.

Prejudice is foreign to you, but please remember that explaining something *once* to others just might not to be enough. Your tendency is to go too fast because you see so clearly. Check carefully to make *sure* all is in correct order. Others tend to be slower than you, so accept this. See them as they are. It's an old "chestnut," but *patience is a virtue.*

NUMBER 24 CHALDEAN

This is a partnership vibration which gives you the ability to take an idea and manifest it into being. The main factor here is love of people and your desire to help.

Because you have had so many problems earlier in life, you now have the experience and understanding to cope with difficult situations before they become serious problems.

You are affectionate and healing to be around. Vibrant and gentle music soothe.

It is true that it's hard for people to get close to you. You are a very private person. Everything you try to accomplish is done with a neat touch and a fine finish. Quality rather than quantity is your method of operation; when you do share intimately it is reciprocal. Your word is your bond. Be flexible in your "word" as many things tend to change swiftly.

Although you are honest, please check thoroughly into other people and their motives to make certain that all they have told you is valid. Don't trust too quickly. Even though a project has an excellent facade, it may be just that, a facade. What is underneath could be very negative for you unless you take the time and effort to check.

NUMBER 25 CHALDEAN

The world does not see how much love you have to give and share. You find intimate, one-to-one relationships best. In your own circle of friends and relatives, you are most comfortable. Dealing with strangers such as required in the dating-game, is not your style.

The power you have to listen carefully and comment

wisely is excellent. The separation of truth from imagination is easy for you to discern. Just like the sphinx of ancient Egypt, you can keep a secret when asked to do so. Little do you realize what a wonderful trait this is in creating close bonds with others. Your need to be honest, loyal, and faithful is rarely deterred from its mark. It's a philosophic part of your nature.

Some of the more delightful aspects of your personality are being a naturally good cook and having a green thumb. Using vibrant color in your home is also a constant joy in your life.

You have a tendency to do and give too much to others and find it difficult to receive in return the care and love you so abundantly give. Often you don't believe a show of affection is real. This is part of your thinking that must be adjusted.

Strange is the aversion you have to people just dropping in to surprise you. The necessity of a phone call before a visit is required. As demanding as you are about proper visitations, the depths of you are as sweet as poetry and soft sentimentality.

As we have discussed, art, social work, psychology, or parapsychology could be excellent vocations.

Listen to advice from within your own being. It's your intuition that will give you guidance. Follow your own instructions in solving problems. You do not have to be affected by outside influences. Just observe silence and listen, and you will find answers.

NUMBER 26 CHALDEAN

You have a strong inclination to save money and handle it wisely. People with this vibration do attain financial abundance. On the other hand, this vibration doesn't buy what is found easily but appears to be too expensive. You search diligently for good buys and bargains. You like having the best and at the same time you get your money's worth.

You sense those who are needy. This may come more in the form of internalization then enlightenment. It is a *must* to be of service to others and be involved in worthwhile causes.

You can blend reality with spirituality, and it works! In escaping from the "rat race," you are able to find, whenever required, a place of solitude within yourself. Go to that special place and revel in this wonderful capacity you have.

NUMBER 27 CHALDEAN

You have a way with the masses. You are strong and extroverted when hearing news of catastrophe. People depend on you for proper decisions. Watch that your compassion does not overwhelm you, especially when you know you can do only so much about a destructive occurrence.

Focus your energies at times when actions bring results. You are a very good person and enjoy playing a part in making this world a better place to live.

You are what people call a "winner." You are less concerned with self-aggrandizement than many other number vibrations. You are a true giver! Your well doesn't run dry. When you give, you do not want or look for anything in return.

The works that you do are most often fruitful. But remember, you cannot carry the burdens of the world on your back. Self-discipline is required in your humanitarian efforts.

NUMBER 28 CHALDEAN

There are many times in your life when you don't know which way to turn even though you may be a take-charge person. This vibration is one that indicates you have great promise. To make the prediction come to pass, that which you achieve both experience-wise and economically has to be squirreled away and kept for the future. Your generous spirit inhibits the saving of funds. You seem to toss away the fruits of your hard work and remarkable ability thinking, "If I can do it now, I can do it again. Let everybody benefit!" You're correct, but the effort must be put out over and over again. You're not being fair to yourself.

Each time you take over and make it happen, the competition is tougher, the laws may change and thwart your efforts, and realization comes too late. Once again you'll be fighting the same battle over and over again. Old Ben Franklin had the right idea: "A penny saved is a penny earned."

NUMBER 29 CHALDEAN

There's an ongoing desire to please other people, to look for approval and be loved. This is why you are so giving, understanding, and compassionate to those in your life.

If you've been feeling a thirst that has been unquenched for some time, you will not find it "out there" in the world. Your hope is based on personal growth. You learn what to achieve one step at a time. It's true, you need to be needed and don't like being alone. You are finding a place within you where you can fulfill this need. You've been disappointed and hurt in life and too often you don't open up because you cannot take rejection or pain.

In needing to be loved you are prone to be chameleon-like, that is, to change your colors to become what the other person wants or needs. In presenting this kind of reaction, you compound the illusion. It's only a matter of time until the cover-up wears off because it isn't real. Then you're back to square one.

Detachment in personal relationships is for you. If life

becomes too sticky, too demanding, you turn your back and don't fight.

Find contentment and fulfillment from within. You already have enough information and tools to plant your seeds properly and harvest a good life.

NUMBER 30 CHALDEAN

You have an excellent mental agility and a wonderful imagination. You can do anything you'd like to do. The object here is to stick to it. Follow through! This will bring your dreams into reality.

You were meant to be in some form of service to help others. The love you feel is unlimited. You can set a fine example by following your inner nature to the best of your ability on a daily basis. Doing this will create a profound effect on all those around you.

You're good with figures, have a fine touch with detail. You can do anything from punching out on a cash register to being a nuclear scientist.

Let go of situations and debris in your life that are no longer useful to you, especially suffocating relationships. Let go. Once you do, don't look back, even mentally.

The past is a canceled check, the present is here and now, and the future is a promissory note. Your best path will be in the here and now as you center on home base.

NUMBER 31 CHALDEAN

Your nature requires you to prepare in advance and have all details planned out meticulously before you act.

You may seem like a fierce opponent, although it's not so. You have the self-control and discipline to harness your indefatigable energies.

Your mind is constantly working even during sleep. Insomnia could be a horrible constant in your life. It's urgent that you exercise your body daily to work off that built-up steam.

Don't get lost in your thoughts of what "could be" to the point you forget the reality of where you are now.

Though you strive for perfection, what was perfect to you last year might not be perfect now. The only thing that changes is change itself. Don't be so rigid. Try to maintain openness and flexibility to transitions. Stop worrying about other people and about their lives. A good key for you is balance and moderation.

Whatever you do you always "carry it off" with dignity.

Your memory is uncanny. You can repeat dates, places, people, poems, and concepts verbatim.

You love discussions merely to see the other person's point of view, then you attack! If it's a light disagreement you always win because you wear out the other party.

NUMBER 32 CHALDEAN

Your sparkling personality brings a combination of all kinds of people from different lands into your life.

It's very fortunate when you allow the creativity of your own thinking pervade that of others. You are the one with the "magic" touch. That's why you attract such a diverse group of people who wish to push their own ideas upon you. Do not permit this. If they stay and do it *your* way, you will find great success. You will not be defeated by others' stupidity and stubbornness. You must not give in.

Your being craves to create and "make it happen." Particularly in marketing new products or places, your unusual sense of finding the proper clientele for your sales campaigns is successful. Your mind searches out that special attraction that will grab the buyer. It's an expertise that works at least ninety percent of the time. Have the faith that *your* way is the *best* way.

NUMBER 33 CHALDEAN

You seem to know what the public wants before they know it. This specifies a good marketing sense. Books you enjoy usually become bestsellers and new trends in fashion colors show in your home and wardrobe before they become popular throughout the world of decor.

Superb taste dominates your preparation of food, cooking, and menu planning. Strange that you rarely prepare the same dish twice in the same way.

Tenderness is a wonderful attribute. You are gentle, caring, and helpful in the extreme to your family and to strangers as well. You are a gracious, kind, and considerate person. This is a trait, by the way, that comes from the maternal side of your family. In one-on-one relationships, you're a master. Perhaps the one overwhelming negative in your character is that insistence to give, give, give.

There are times when part of you cannot put up with screaming and loud noises. The only time it's permissible is when you are carrying on yourself!

You find it so much easier to care deeply and feel for others' pain. Try learning how to receive by internalizing this question about yourself. Meditate on this; it's important that you have a better understanding. You'll find more happiness in allowing others to give, give, give to you.

Many of your problems originate with your ongoing efforts to influence other peoples' lives. If you think about it, "people have to do what they have to do!" You have that realization, you do understand this. Almost never do you judge or condemn; you just get too personally involved. Let go! Stop worrying about your future and start to enjoy what you have right *now*. A wise man once said, "the past is gone, the future hasn't come, there is only the *now*."

NUMBER 34 CHALDEAN

You yearn to be and often are the person in the back room pushing the buttons behind the scenes to make the whole production work. The public rarely sees you. Those people who are up front and on the stage know the show has gone as smooth as silk and they attribute it to you. You do not require a pat on the back as most do. That it has gone well is sufficient. It's for your own self-respect to do your best always. Everything you do is planned and finalized before the first step is taken.

The insight you have is a combination to open the vault of your world. You have the ability to know what the public wants before they do.

So-called Luck appears to be a highly intuitive gift, or through psychic phenomena you "know." Your first reactions are astoundingly accurate.

The rain tends to have a magical effect upon you.

You have wisdom beyond your years—follow it.

Trust yourself!

NUMBER 35 CHALDEAN

It would be marvelous if life were a bowl of cherries. Everything perfect, everything unmarred. If you will face the truth, you *know* it's just not that way.

This vibration carries serious warnings for the future. Remember, it is under your control to weave your own patterns by choice. It is not what you say but what you do. Your deeds in life are what count.

It is not a good idea for you to have partners or associates who have the same amount of legal control in a business or venture that you share.

When you listen to advice, be certain it's from people

who have your best interests at heart.

Your basic nature goes back to the "sweat of your brow" theory. This *cannot* change. Carefully weigh all things that seem a snap or get-rich-quick schemes. It won't work for you. Be careful at all times when others join you in moneymaking opportunities. You have to do it your way with no outside guidance. What you personally deduct *will* be correct. Partnerships are out.

NUMBER 36 CHALDEAN

The world has prepared a pulpit or lectern from which you should proselytize or speak.

Your methods are almost evangelical. You are persuasive and demanding. This inherent ability to move the masses can be done with much less fire and brimstone. Your anger or rage is not always an aid in your work.

Relent for your own good. Your fine qualities to make a better world for others should bring you joy, not frustration. You should have learned by now what an altrusitic person you are. Everyone you deal with knows you only want to give happiness and you expect nothing in return. Your results in any work you undertake will be successful if you learn the first and foremost lesson for your superb personality; self-discipline.

Helping others can not only be a thankless task but a frustrating experience of spinning your wheels. Your nature carries your disappointment inward. This is not good. If just one thing you say reaches the mentality of the suffering, you've won. Remember always, even the greatest of leaders cannot change the world.

NUMBER 37 CHALDEAN

Your leadership qualities encourage relationships with a variety of people. Each person feels it's on a one-to-one basis. Though your friends may not know each other, you have the gifted facility to share each of their lives in a beautiful, unique, and supportive way.

You are the center of the wheel and are able to create "spokes" on that wheel that make each person a special part of your life.

Your way tends to be right and you see things through other people's eyes. Through this clear perspective, your true vision is unlimited.

Frequently you need to recharge and renew yourself in solitude.

NUMBER 38 CHALDEAN

If this number vibration takes over your personality, it will lead absolutely to major uncertainties, treachery, and deception. It's a very difficult vibration to overcome unless you are aware of what could happen if you allow yourself the freedom to be a slave to total negativity! If so, you will reap the very worst of life's rewards. There will be many trials, legal as well as real, in your life. Unexpected dangers will be thrown in your path.

With this awareness, you *must* abide by the morality of life. You know and have known for quite some time if you think and act positively, you'll create the proper vibrations to overcome this negative inclination you have. Please, be careful of your actions and thinking. Be the very best you can when dealing with others! Do this now. Exhibit understanding and compassion in all things. Keep your own being "up."

NUMBER 39 CHALDEAN

This is a unique vibration. It is completely devoid of looking for monetary gain and you will show total lack of concern if there is "no money." Your caring about material things is controlled by your own mental outlook. It is more important to analyze all those you meet. There is a private need within for deep introspection to have the answers to all questions about others' personalities. You ask yourself, "What do they really mean?"

You've got to watch that superior attitude of yours. Your marvelous ability of deduction can sometimes be way off the mark. Give others the benefit of having learned how to hide their deepest thoughts and feelings.

Basing your knowledge of people on this highly advanced mental plane you live on can be very disappointing. You have got to develop that *gut feeling*, not go on your mental processes alone.

NUMBER 40 CHALDEAN

You are pedantic, specific, and are a perfectionist when you are planning a project. It's important to you that all details be carefully attended to before you begin.

This special part of your personality sends out the wrong messages to those who don't agree with you. You are not fierce. You enjoy listening to a logical argument. Unfortunately, many don't have your perfect self-control and discipline.

Insomnia may be one of your difficult problems to overcome. Invisible activity keeps you awake, even when you are ready to sleep. The old-fashioned remedy of drinking warm milk, chamomile, or decaffinated tea could be very helpful. The best effort is to quiet your ever-working mind.

Readjust your thinking to envision the clean lines of a triangle or a square, just the shapes; that also may help.

You should be thankful that time or varied incidents can change your thinking. You are not so inflexible that intelligent transition is not possible.

Dignified and independent describes the inner you. Memory is a plus factor in advancing your career. The details that pass others by stay entrenched in your mind.

The debating team, at any stage of your life—high school, college or post-graduate education—is a must for your number 40 Chaldean. In fact, if life were an ongoing series of debates, you would be a very, very content person.

NUMBER 41 CHALDEAN

The structure of your personality is like a meeting of the United Nations. You need constant stimulation. You need to create innovative patterns of conduct. It's only in this fashion you are truly happy.

As soon as life shifts into a low gear of activity, you begin to wilt. Like a magnificent hothouse flower, your mind and body commence a depressive plunge. At times like this you can stir up other activities in the creative area of the arts. You may or may not paint, draw, or play a musical instrument like a virtuoso, but you can participate in events to raise money for charity or for a particular person that needs help.

Your way is usually the most successful, unique way to accomplishment. In moments like this you need to be the obstinate renegade that sees success in new and exciting endeavors that will benefit all.

NUMBER 42 CHALDEAN

Your vibration carries you to the highest and most respected circles. Socially those who are the very "tops" in rank and success are somehow attracted to you.

The opposite sex always brings you gain through love. Intuitively you make the correct moves in the sensual areas of your life. The opposite gender is most delightful and sharing time with them is one of your favorite hobbies. Rarely is your guard up. You're disarming, flattering, and fun. There are times when your partners in romance misinterpret your attention. They equate it to being in love! Those problems are not difficult for you to handle. With suave and compassionate words, you make yourself understood swiftly. "I really like you, you're an interesting person. We must get to know each other better!"

When you're angry, your charm and pleasant personality go haywire. You fight and will not permit opposition. You will fight vehemently for others' honor or their right to be and say what's good for them.

Are you the elusive white knight in shining armor? Are you the representation of Athena, the mythological goddess of the hunt? Why not? You could be if you believe it!

NUMBER 43 CHALDEAN

You build your life brick by brick starting at the bottom, like a pyramid on a strong foundation.

Life is real and life is earnest. Keep that pyramid without a crack in it. Only then can there be no more pain. Always remember, do not allow anyone else's sadness to enter your life. Commiserate, but keep sorrow at arm's length.

Do not depend on others. Be self-contained. Once you have cut the cords of dependency, one at a time, softly and gently, you will find a greater understanding of your own nature.

Your inner strength is phenomenal. Picture a merry-go-around and you're on a beautifully decorated horse, holding on to the pole. The merry-go-round is circling, you're going up and down on your steed, and the pole is just there, solid, firm. Hold on to the pole at all times. This is the stable part of your inner strength. Whatever you see as the merry-go-round turns is transitional, just hold on to the pole and enjoy the ride. For you, it is always just the beginning.

NUMBER 44 CHALDEAN

You must keep very busy and active. Your mind is interested in *how* things work. Detach yourself from everything around you, relax, and let that wonderful brain of yours do its work.

There doesn't seem to be enough time in the day to accomplish all the things you wish to do.

Remember all those incomplete projects? Don't worry about them, just have fun and do not get lost. Let others attend to the details at your direction.

Fun is an important part of life's activity—learning, growing, being kind to yourself!

NUMBER 45 CHALDEAN

This vibration promises authority, power, and command. It warrants that reward comes from your intellectual thinking, productive thinking. The creative facility of your vibration is forever sewing seeds of better and faster ways of doing things.

It is also a particularly exciting vibration that carries a fine promise of success in future events.

This vibration relates closely to the greatest secrets of

the occult, and people like you are intrigued with all the religions in the universe. You may choose to fulfill your destiny as a priest, clergyman, or rabbi.

NUMBER 46 CHALDEAN

You lead the parade. In the ranks are people of all colors and creeds. You have the remarkable ability to encourage all people to join forces behind you. You are a born diplomat and convince the world that each person in your life is of particular importance to you.

The dynamism of your innate nature is a magnet, attracting all to the belief that you agree with their point of view. You have the mind of a politician and the soul of a saint.

It may be frustrating, even to you, that what you see as a solution to many issues is correct. It can be difficult to be right so often.

Functioning in top gear most of your life, if you are middle-aged, you most likely have learned you must retire from activity several times a year. If you are younger, learn this lesson now.

The inner you can lead to an exhausted outer you. Renewal and a recharging of your miraculous energies can only occur in solitude.

Retreat when you feel yourself winding down. Take a sabbatical even if it's seven hours or seven days.

NUMBER 47 CHALDEAN

You want to *hear* from people about their feelings concerning you. Craving affection, touching, holding, loving is a wondrous part of you but others are less apt to fulfill that immense need. You can recall so many cries to which there was no response. All the world ignored the need within them. Sad, but you learned most of the facts as you grew up. You were the one who felt this deep-seated desire and others just did not realize how much they had to give. This conduct has been modified, your awareness is much sharper, your demands much less.

You exhibit nearperfectionist neatness, orderliness, and precision. The miraculous computer in your brain allows the information to collate, then prints out perfect answers. Follow the result and you'll rarely make a mistake.

Often you hold bothersome conduct by others inside until you are ready to explode. It's better to express your distress at the start. A relationship must be aligned correctly before there can be any reconciliation. Be your own navigator. Always come back to your home port; listen to the voice within.

Look for changes in the direction of your life. It will be different than in the past. It's fine as long as you feel good about it. Beware of overdependence on situations around you. Maintain self-reliance at all times. There is a tendency to blow a problem out of proportion, giving it more importance than deserved. This will always brings a downfall. You've got a great sense of humor—use it!

NUMBER 48 CHALDEAN

You are so very ambitious that you do not ever want to be in a subordinate position. Your "rise in the world" is the only satisfactory way in your lifetime.

Your excellent ability to take command is based upon your love of order and discipline. Not only that, but you will readily obey orders from the *boss,* if he or she is a person you respect.

You excel in positions of authority in the military.

If trust and responsibility is required, your vibration is very conscientious in carrying out your duties.

If anything, the desire or possibility to be a dictator is always there. This personality flaw must be watched carefully or it could be disastrous in what otherwise would be a very successful career. That tendency you have to squirm under the least bit of restraint must be overcome. You can and will win with more self-control.

NUMBER 49 CHALDEAN

This is a lonely vibration and represents a self-contained person who will not bend, a person who refuses to be a little more flexible even knowing that being unbending will hinder progress in this material world.

Your vibration has a very distinctive character. You view life from opposite angles than most and see things that other number vibrations miss.

You are not intentionally quarrelsome, yet you attract opposition, sometimes creating business enemies.

Instinctively you rebel against rules and regulations but are successful in reversing statutes in government and solidifying community relations.

You are very positive in your views and unconventional in your follow-through. When involved in charitable causes you make enough changes so that people are stirred to action with no compensation to them, they work just for the cause.

Although you do not make friends easily, you are attracted to people who really "don't care" what you do or how you do it as long as you share yourself with them. It's an unconditional love whether friendship or romance.

NUMBER 50 CHALDEAN

It's a strong vibration for you to handle being so versatile and able to place yourself on any ladder to success of projects or occupations that attract you. You create confusion in your own mind. Versatility can be a curse unless you "grab the bull by the horns" and get moving on one thing. There's a tendency to be easily swayed over what you think you should be doing. Choose one of the many, many outlets open to you and *get started*.

Many times, you ponder along the way, not taking advantage of the *now* to further your goals. Press yourself forward. You would not have chosen the avenue you are on if it didn't excite your imagination in the first place.

You have no difficulty making friends. Don't concern yourself if some relationships are not long lasting. Party people are out for fun and if their actions and style are your delight, you must wait until the light of day to see what they are really like in the game of survival in living life.

There is a tendency to exhaust yourself dallying in many projects at the same time. This can push you into a depression. Avoid this tendency. Watch your own stress level. Keep busy but be careful not to overdo.

NUMBER 51 CHALDEAN

The obstinate you does not easily become revealed to your "subjects." Somehow, you're the royalty and the rest of the world the masses. An unyielding will becomes the *you* others thought never existed. Then quite suddenly (and often) you do an about-face and are in love!

As if a light switch were turned on, you become a devoted slave; giving, giving, giving to the adored one. That *one* chosen out of the masses of your admirers. If it were not such a serious turn-on to you, it would be comical to those who observe you. The queen bee or king of the road is in the slave dock and is breathless, awaiting the adored one's next command.

Suddenly this bower of flowers and instant romance begins to falter! Why? You *imagine* the object of your dreams and sexual fantasies talked too nicely to another, winked his or her eye at another, and jealousy flares. This is your major weakness.

It's a problem to take care of every aspect of your special person; fulfill human needs, provide luxury cars, give special expensive gifts, and then *they turn on you.* Imagined or not, the fling is over. No returns! It's done, they're out.

The wonderful part of it is that you're ready to try again. You are never resentful, just somewhat sad over your lover's lack of appreciation!

NUMBER 52 CHALDEAN

What style! What individuality! It's not easy for people to fully understand you. Your extreme independence shines through at all times, creating an attitude of aloofness from the world. It's a shell that cannot be cracked, an adamant nature that *can* see all sides of a situation but refuses to accept any but your personal interpretation.

Travel to foreign lands, by train or plane, whether in your imagination or in reality, is a joy in life. To be tethered to the earth is like being in a straightjacket. Reading books of adventure, detective stories, or tales of sleuths like Sherlock Holmes are your wings of fantasy to fly.

The true happiness in your life is not conversation with others but being alone in your thoughts to travel along a steep mountain path or being equipped to go seven leagues beneath the sea. Jules Verne, the famous author, could be your hero.

You are a true philosopher in the establishment. With proper credentials you could teach in high academic circles. Commenting on the various areas of life and how we all must meet fate head-on and deal with your own lives is one of your favorite pastimes. You never force these ideals or ideas about "what's right" on others. Not because you are so fixed a humanitarian, but because you really *don't care.* That's okay too!

NUMBER 53 CHALDEAN

"Why am I so lonely?" "Why am I so misunderstood?"
It's the major puzzle in life and is never answered. At first
you get a glimpse of *why*. It holds for a moment and then,
so fleeting, it is gone!

If you want the truth, accept the fact that you are destined
to play some important role on the stage of life. It is not
satisfactory to be second lead or an extra. Your being requires you be a star. The concept of *Fate* is your deepest
understanding of the mysteries of life. "What is meant to
be will be!" You can and will always do your best to be
the best you can be but underneath your consciousness you
know it's all in the cards. It's prewoven into a tapestry of
life without your control. Feeling this way, you accept life,
its disappointments and joys. "It is my destiny!"

Religious fanaticism could be a downfall if you allow it.
If your choice of faith in God is created only by the ritual
of established religions or if you choose to be a lover of
God in Nature (Pantheism), it doesn't matter. Your way is
the only way. With this attitude, especially where religion
is concerned, you could make bitter enemies. You cannot
seem to let up on preaching! It's your way or no way.

You really don't care what people think but are deeply
effected by famine in the world, the homeless, and all the
social disgraces we have on this bountiful planet.

Why can't everybody share? It's not fair for some to
have so much and others nothing. Rather than express these
thoughts, you make anonymous contributions to organiza-
tions or families or individuals who need your help.

NUMBER 54 CHALDEAN

It's as if you are always on the razor's edge of life. Move one way, you know you'll lose. Move the other, and you'll dislike or maybe resent that choice! You have a special way of compromising with yourself. Always eager to have the best of all worlds, your penchant for delay works well for you. By creating a "crater" or a "nothingness" about a definite decision to be made, Fate steps in and does it for you. It *always* works that way.

Often you can find a life companion in late youth. Someone with whom you have ongoing surprises in life with every year that passes in your relationship. That's what keeps you together. It's usually a person of extreme independence, who does not cling to you and who, quite often, has a successful career of his or her own.

You do not object to a lover or mate to work long hours in their business or profession, but let them be late or hurried or too tired in a rendezvous with you and you can turn on them like a centipede with a thousand legs who stings with a sharp tongue. This trait you have could create fathoms of separation from your object of love. Be more understanding in this area. Try to realize that *once* is not *always*.

NUMBER 55 CHALDEAN

Life can be and most often is a wonderful mixture of many interests. There's an abundance of need for you to be continually learning, always searching. Because of this, there's never a definitive pattern of what area will grasp your interest next. This unpredictability is one of the exciting mysteries of your personality. It's fortunate you have so many interests. So many appealing new dimensions of thought to dip into. From politics to penmanship, you're with it and do surely live in the *now*.

Straight as an arrow, never dancing around the truth, your directness is sometimes startling. So few people really want to hear the truth. But that does not stop you from "saying it as it is!"

You're a fun-loving person and are able to mimic others. You put images and concepts of ideas and people together very quickly.

The numerous acquaintances that flow in and out of your life are like a United Nations assembly. People from all walks of life. Wealthy, poor, all colors, all ages, and you possess a grand attitude of being unprejudiced in your contacts. This seemingly impossible clutter of people in your life becomes somewhat restricted when contact is made. The reasons for this are often well hidden. Not holding on to objects or people is a firm part of your psyche. One of the important parts of yourself you must attend to is that you are bored easily. Perhaps at times your patience is too short, magnifying your discontent with others who think more slowly. You may not show it but you'll act to remove that which you see as impediments to your joy of living.

CHAPTER ELEVEN

Summary of Your Numbers of Destiny

In any new adventure or after any unique change in our lives, many of us are stirred, some even to the point of wondering, "What if, what if I had known about my keys sooner? Would my destiny have been different?"

If we were fortunate enough to give you an additional slant on your life, a strange but delightful perspective of all the great opportunities surrounding you, we'll be very grateful. Would your destiny have been different if you'd read this earlier? No, we don't think so. Why? Because *Now* is the time you were meant to take another look at your life. Because *Now* is the time to begin a campaign that will enhance your days. Make life more fulfilling.

Numerology, or any new areas you discover and inspect and choose to make a part of yourself, can only instill a positive response. The sages say, "First, know thyself."

MIND MEETS BODY...
HEALTH MEETS HAPPINESS...
SPIRIT MEETS SERENITY...

In his writings, spiritual advisor Edgar Cayce counseled thousands with his extraordinary, yet practical guidance to the mind/body/spirit connection. Now, the Edgar Cayce series, based on actual readings by the renowned psychic, can provide you with insights in the search for understanding and meaning in life.

KEYS TO HEALTH: The Promise and Challenge of Holism
Eric A. Mein, M.D.
_____ 95616-9 $4.99 U.S./$5.99 CAN.

REINCARNATION: Claiming Your Past, Creating Your Future
Lynn Elwell Sparrow
_____ 95754-8 $4.99 U.S./$5.99 CAN.

DREAMS: Tonight's Answers for Tomorrow's Questions
Mark Thurston, Ph.D.
_____ 95771-8 $5.50 U.S./$6.50 CAN.